Wallace-Homestead

Price Guide to
Toys

By Robert W. Miller

Published by
Wallace-Homestead Book Company
P. O. Box BI
Des Moines, Iowa 50304

Photography by
Tom Needham
Panama City, Florida

Library of Congress
Catalog Card No.: 75-41895
ISBN: 0-87069-161-9

COVER PHOTO: SCHOENHUT ELEPHANT, multi-jointed, late 1880s, **$45-$55.** MARX "WONDER CYCLIST," tin mechanical windup, early 1900s, 9" high, **$85-$95.** STUFFED "BUNNY RABBIT," tin mechanical windup, mohair-covered, early 1900s, 11½" high, **$35-$45.** DUMP-ING OR TUMBLER CART, painted wood pull toy, made by Ehrich Brothers, New York, New York, 1882, **$85-$100.**

TABLE OF CONTENTS

ACKNOWLEDGMENTS

Mrs. Margaret Reinhold Crawbuck

An historic house and a collection of yesterday's playthings. Together they exhibit the love and devotion of those people responsible for making the Museum of Yesterday's Toys possible.

Through the preservation of the historic Rodrigues-Avero-Sanchez house by Margaret Reinhold Crawbuck and her late husband, Walter, and the entire toy and doll collection of these two devoted people, Americans today can view one of the world's finest collections of playthings.

The museum is located on St. George Street in the old, walled city of St. Augustine, Florida. Its director, William Jordan Daniell, was the driving force behind the present-day restoration of the St. George Street area. One of the world's leading authorities on Spanish influence in American history, Bill Daniell refused to take no for an answer in 1950; and today, those of us who appreciate our heritage owe this devoted and determined man our undying gratitude.

In the days when this area of St. Augustine was about to be demolished to make way for modern concrete and glass office buildings, Dr. Daniell rallied his forces. He suffered occasional setbacks to be sure, but today one need only stroll along this oldest street in North America to visualize what love, devotion, and teamwork can accomplish.

With humility and gratitude I thank Mrs. Crawbuck, Bill Daniell and his competent staff, and, last but not least, Sunshine, a polo-pony-sized great dane, who with her master, Jacques (Jack) Bolduc, pitched in beyond the call of duty to make this book possible.

God bless!

Robert W. Miller

INTRODUCTION

The prices listed in this *Wallace-Homestead Price Guide to Toys* are average retail prices that reflect the age and condition of a toy. They are based on my experience and that of museums and dealers throughout the United States.

It is virtually impossible to quote exact prices because of the nation's economy at this time. Every effort has been made to arrive at sensible prices; but prices vary from region to region, making it impossible to set one price. This is why this guide gives two prices for each item—a high and a low. The average price is somewhere in between.

The price of old toys has skyrocketed in recent years. Although every effort has been made to eliminate errors, neither I nor the publisher can be held responsible for mistakes in the prices given in this guide.

Always keep in mind the condition of a toy, its age, and its availability in today's market. Whenever possible, buy, sell, or trade toys in person. Like coins, don't expect the toy you buy by mail to measure up to its advertised condition. If you don't specify what you are looking for, look out! When cheated, notify postal authorities immediately. Full-page ads in publications on antiques and collectibles are fine if you know the advertiser and what **you** are doing.

I have tried hard to give you a book with lots of photos, lots of prices, and lots of advice. Now I welcome your questions, suggestions, and criticisms. Address your letters to me in care of the publisher, and please enclose a self-addressed stamped envelope. Then, be patient!

Thank you for buying my book.

ABOUT THE AUTHOR

Prominently listed in International Who's Who In Art and Antiques and a long-standing member of the Appraisers Association of America, Robert W. Miller is recognized internationally as one of the world's leading authorities on antiques. His books are accepted as standard reference works by libraries, historical societies, antique dealers and private collectors. Host of his own television show, he's appeared on many national "talk shows." When Mr. Miller isn't lecturing here and abroad he can be found on the Gulf of Mexico in his Bertram 31, seeking out the elusive sailfish and white marlin.

PLAYTHINGS: THEIR INFLUENCE ON MANKIND

Generally speaking, a plaything is any article prized more for its charm or interest than for its utilitarian qualities. Without playthings we still would live a primitive life in this 20th century.

As long as 4,000 years ago, children played with toys much like those played with by today's children: marbles, dolls, wooden and stone balls. And more than one invention that helped mankind move up the ladder of civilization resulted from an adult watching a child at play. Thomas Edison, for example, gave us motion pictures by simply running a piece of zoetrope film through a child's magic lantern he had electrified.

Burial mounds dating from the Stone Age have given up crudely made dolls carved from stone. Other objects indicate how much time a loving parent, centuries ago, devoted to making a toy for a child to play with. Nowhere in the back rivers of time do we find a complete lack of playthings.

If in the first creation life was cruel and all too short, the elders loved their children. When a respite from the fight for survival presented itself, parents carved or molded things for the youngsters.

Toys in Early Civilizations

As time passed, settled communities developed where there was an abundance of water, timber, and game. Possessions were accumulated, and it was only natural that the residents of these settlements made things with their hands as the need for a particular item arose. High on this list were playthings for the children. Riverbanks yielded clay for pots and sand for the children to play in. Pull toys and carts were made for the younger set 3,000 years before Christ.

The opening of ancient graves and burial mounds in Egypt and Mesopotamia has produced bird whistles, animals with nodding heads, and children's beads. During the same period, Chinese children entertained themselves with shadowy figures made from wax. Bronze was used for making small animals and figurines. And it wasn't always the adult who did the creating. A small boy, bored with tossing pebbles into a stream, might have whittled a stick for throwing at rabbits and other small game. If it worked, his parents quickly adapted it to their own use.

Competitive Games

Almost 100 years before Anno Domini (A.D.), olympian games were held in Greece. As these games of sport spread to other parts of the world, young men and women competed against each other using weights of stone and javelins made from shaven pieces of wood. Knuckles wrapped with horse or cow hide sufficed as boxing gloves. About 30 B.C., the Olympic Games, as they had come to be called, were so important in Europe that people going to or from Greece were protected by a truce when crossing hostile lands.

When the early Christians went into hiding to avoid being killed for their refusal to worship the Roman emperor, they made crude toys to keep their children quiet. The Romans themselves had been making alabaster balls, bone dice, and glass marbles for many years, and it becomes a bit confusing when these items are excavated in different parts of England, left behind when the Romans departed for home.

A transition Period for Man and Toys

As the Dark Ages in Europe came and went, time, which has a habit of healing all wounds, showed the citizenry that there was indeed light at the end of the tunnel. Anglo-Saxons joined the ranks of Christianity, and the scholars wrote of this momentous event on a new substance called parchment. Through it all, the children enjoyed archery, emulating their elders who rode horses bedecked with ornate saddles and stirrups to match.

About 620 A.D. China was considered the most civilized nation in the world. The Persians busied themselves learning a new game called chess. Meanwhile, in England, a variety of toys were being sold at the many fairs. And sad but true, so were the children, whom parents offered to the Irish for use as slaves. Canute II, the king of England and Denmark, stopped this nonsense in the 11th century when he sailed up the Thames.

The merry-go-round first appeared in England, as did ice skates. Dolls with paper dresses, high-flying kites, and other assorted goodies amused the Chinese during the Sung dynasty (960-1276 A.D.). On the Continent, stationery was the new fad, and more and more people learned how to write. Stationers sold stationery from a stall that stayed in one place.

An Infatuation with Toy Soldiers

Through the ages, toy soldiers have always held a fascination for children from 9 to 90. When the lords of medieval castles became bored with dice and chess, they rode off to make war. The children stayed behind to play "fighting" and other games that one day would stand them in good stead when it came their turn to go to war.

By the 14th century, quintain, a popular game of the day, was played on horseback, in a boat, or on foot. The object: To put your jousting pole through a hole in a board or through a metal ring hanging from a post.

During this same period, Italians, young and old, amused themselves with a game called bocce—lawn bowling with wooden or stone balls on a long, narrow court, usually made of hardened clay. And while Leonardo da Vinci was busy making models of flying birds, the children of Italy played with toy windmills and animals with wagging heads.

In Germany and Holland, metal toys and miniature crossbows were the playthings of the day.

So it went. Trinkets, knickknacks, ornaments, baubles, call them what you will. All had a pronounced influence on civilization today. It was son mimicking father, daughter copying mother.

Kinds of Toys

Actually, playthings—call them toys if you will—fall into two basic categories:

1. Representational—intended to stimulate rather than to be used for a practical purpose.

2. Non-representational—intended to encourage manual or muscular dexterity and group integration by the use of such objects as balls, tops, or jump ropes.

Too many people think about toys as objects associated with children. Think about an adult native in a foreign land seeing for the first time a mirror, or shoes, or most any artifact of modern civilization. A plaything? A toy?

Toy Trading

In 16th century Europe, cabinets of toy collections were the fashion, the cabinets sometimes being more ornately carved than the toys themselves. Tennis (tenysplaye), football, and other competitive sports of the day were enjoyed by one and all.

The greatest toy trading center in medieval Europe was Nuremberg, Germany. An imperial city, by 1530 it commanded the attention of all Europe. Several hundred years and a few wars later this same great city became the center of controversy among free men.

By the late 1500s, if America was still in swaddling clothes, Europe was ablaze with the latest fashions and newest things in toys. Kings, queens, maids, chauffers, and butlers all purchased toys for their children. Even William Shakespeare wrote about English boys who played hookey from school and spun their tops, raced their toy boats in the park fountains, and enjoyed a day away from the three R's.

Toys Come to America

By 1700 English toys found their way to the American colonies, where door-to-door salesmen peddled chap-books for children.

Because most crown heads of Europe were interested in toys, many sets of miniature Meissen tea services, snuff boxes, and dinner services were produced for the powers that were. Though quite fragile, the porcelains have long outlasted the royal families.

Ten years before our ancestors told King George II what he could do with it, most colonial nurseries had a horse-on-wheels, lettered bricks, and cup-and-ball games. Shortly thereafter, bells and rattles in the hands of children made almost as much noise as the "indians" who tossed bale after bale of tea into Boston's harbor.

During the French Revolution, children were given toy guillotines with which they could decapitate toy figures depicting French aristocrates. If this was considered educational at the time, somewhere along the line the thought or reasoning behind it all was lost forever.

In the 19th century wooden toys gave way to metal toys and then to brass and mechanical toys, especially after the secret of stamping sheet metal was discovered. More than one young man who served his apprenticeship in toy manufacturing went on to the manufacturing of automobiles, steel, and railroads.

About 1840, penny dreadfuls made their mark on the English and American markets. Ghoulish tales of murder—and worse— were read to children at bedtime, a flickering lamp adding to the suspense and mystery. Anyone who wonders why our grandparents were afraid of the dark and insisted that a light be left burning in the hall has only to read a penny dreadful on a rainy night in an empty house.

Exhibitions Promote Toy Sales

No doubt the Paris exhibitions of 1844 and the Crystal Palace exhibition of 1851 did more to promote toys worldwide than anything prior to those dates. Name the toy. It was on display!

The year 1852 saw toys made of copper; and surprisingly, American manufacturers were exporting toys and dolls made of rubber to England. By 1860 aluminum toys were on the market. No one paid too much attention as the children played with miniature pots, pans, and tableware, but it didn't take long for the manufacturers of kitchenware to take note of this lightweight metal.

Nine years later a product called celluloid was invented that would revolutionize the toy industry. Amazingly, use of this highly flammable compound of pyroxylin and camphor in the toy-making industry was not banned until 99 years later.

The effect aluminum and celluloid had on the development of our civilization was unbelievable. Once again children's toys were put to a utilitarian use.

In 1870, millions, young and old, skated out to greet the new year, this time on roller skates. Small watches and toys were being made from a product called pinchbeck in honor of the man who discovered it, Christopher Pinchbeck, a London toy seller. The alloy—25 percent zinc and 75 percent copper —was easy to work with and stood up fairly well under the brutal treatment children subjected their toys to.

Toys in the 20th Century

As the 19th century gave way to the 20th, a great queen, Victoria, was dead. Parents, reluctant to allow their offspring to play with tin toys, still purchased the beautifully carved and painted wooden toys from India. Among the other toys popular with the children of the early 20th century were rocking horses, humming tops, lead soldiers, music boxes, and doll houses.

By 1914 rattling sabers once again echoed across Europe. When World War I began, anything marked "Made in Germany" was in for a hard time, particularly in England and France. It would be quite some time before German-made toys would be accepted as playthings, and then only those toys not depicting war.

Meanwhile, a strange toy called a pogo stick proved singularly responsible for breaking more than a few arms and legs. Built like a broomstick, it had platforms on each side for the feet and a heavy spring that enabled the user to hop up and down like a rabbit with a hot coal in its bloomers. Oh, those 1920s.

Not long thereafter the heavy, black clouds of war once again scudded across the land. In England the children were forbidden to pick up anything out-of-doors because the air force of the maniac paper hanger was dropping tiny bombs that looked like butterflies. Capable of blowing off a leg, or worse, too many children became their victims.

After World War II plastic replaced wood and tin, and the emphasis in toy-making shifted from quality to quantity with Hong Kong leading the way to Junksville.

Antique Playthings

Any plaything made before 1890 is now considered an antique. The number of toy collectors around the world is staggering. Obviously demand exceeds supply, so be careful. Many reproductions, some good enough to fool even the experts, are flooding world markets.

One of the finest toy collections in the world is located in the Museum of Yesterday's Toys on St. George Street in St. Augustine, Florida. Other toy museums are listed elsewhere in this book.

Always remember: If you don't know your toys, know your toy dealer.

Good hunting!

GLOSSARY OF TOY TERMS

—A—

aloutte: First flying toy; France, 1787. A tug on the string sent the butterfly or whatever soaring off the end of a stick.

anchor blocks: First stone building blocks for children; invented by a Dr. Richter, Austria, early 1800s.

apple mill, whizzgig, water cutter: Similar to modern-day yoyos.

articulas: Moving toys displaying people at work or play; movement derived from a heat turbine, steam engine, etc.

—B—

barrel spring: Part of a clockwork windup; always used on Lehmann toys.

battledore: Early form of badmitton racket; usually made of parchment.

bell toy: When pulled or pushed, bell(s) ring(s). Punch and Judy is a famous bell toy. Invented in Germany, 1790s, early 1800s.

bellow toys: Activate the bellows, birds pecked, people moved; at least 1700s. Bellows mounted inside animals around 1830. The lie-down, sit-up sound appeared about 1860.

bilboquet (cup and ball): Catch the ball in a cup or on the end of a pointed stick; originated in Victorian England.

Blenheim Palace: The birthplace of Sir Winston Churchill in Warwickshire; contains a marvelous display of Lucotte soldiers.

bosses, bonces, kings: Medieval marbles.

bounce toy: A jointed figure danced on a wire when the board to which the wire was attached was tapped with the hand.

Boxer Rebellion: A Chinese secret society (1900s) whose badge was a clenched fist (boxer). A toy involving those who took part in putting down the rebellion was made by Lehmann.

brass toy: Alloy of tin and copper; expensive to make unless cast. Ancient toys (India) were made of brass.

Britain, W., and Sons: Famous as producers of toy soldiers; England.

Britannia: A cheap pewter-like metal used to make toys.

bull-roarer: A piece of wood attached to a string that made a rumbling noise when whirled rapidly; originally used by early Egyptians to stimulate the rain god.

—C—

cabane: A game—put the marbles in the center of the ring; French, early 19th century.

candle-trow: Some say it was the original Christmas tree; decorated with many candles; ancient, English.

cast iron: A hard, unmalleable pig iron; made by casting into a mold.

cheapjacks: English toy sellers who hawked their wares in London's Regent Park on Sundays or at Holborn Circus, etc., early 19th century.

China spinning top: Made from conch shells that are leveled down at the head and weighted with lead at the tip.

clockwork toy: Early type of windup mechanism; used in clocks, etc.

cock horse: "To ride a cock horse"—to ride astride, stiff, and erect.

cocotte: Paper-folding; to make a figure by folding a piece of paper.

comic character toy: Toy based on a newspaper, radio, television, or movie character —Howdy Doody, Dick Tracy, etc.

—D—

daedaleum: See *Zoetrope*.

diablo: Originally an Asian game, consisting of two sticks with a string attached. You balanced a spool-like object on the string.

dryland boat: Usually with wheels, for indoor play.

—E—

electric toy: Operated by electricity.

emigrant (or emigrette): Earliest known form of modern yoyo.

—F—

flats: Military toys made in Nuremberg; figures cast so they were embossed on one side only, end of 18th century.

friction toy: Heavy flywheel attached to toy made it go.

—G—

GBNE: Trademark of Bing of Nuremberg; made early hot-air machines.

Golliwog: Grotesque black doll.

goose: A travel game; in many forms over the years; more than 400 years old.

Guckkastenbild: Peep-box picture show, German, 18th century.

—H—

Hoops: Used to reinforce wine kegs, etc., about 15th century. Some kid rolled one and the trundling game began.

—I—

—J—

johnny jump-ups: A jack-in-the-box.

jolly boys: In Westmoreland, England, these lads visit local homes on Easter where they enact an ancient play involving eggs and beer. Walking in a circle, they sing a rhyme by which the drama is introduced.

jumping jack: Dancing figure on a string; also called Pantins, Hampelmanns, or Zappelmanns.

—K—

kaleidoscope: Three mirrors form a triangle within the confines of the hexagonal case. When the case is turned, different patterns appear.

—L—

ladder walker: A block or other object comes down the ladder, rung by rung, end over end; usually weighted at one end.

lithograph: Cheap picture paper applied on wooden toys; also cardboard and tin.

live animal toys: Toy operated by placing live bird or mouse in cage; when animal moved, toy operated.

—M—

Maerklin, Bing and Carette: German toymakers who produced most of the toy ships in the 19th century.

Mah-Jongg: A game played with ivory tiles. J. C. Babcock named the game in 1924. The Chinese have played it for thousands of years.

marbles: Originated about 200 A.D.; came to medieval England from the low countries; introduced in America about 1890.

meccano: The abbreviation of "mechanics made easy," a trade name used in England since 1907 by the Hornby system.

mechanical: Toy that operates on gravity; no motor.

mechanical banks: When a coin was inserted, figure(s) did something.

mechanical windup: Later version of clockwork windup.

monopoly: World's most popular game next to you-know-what; invented by George Darrow, 1933.

—N—

nest dolls: A series of carved wooden dolls, each fitting into the other.

Newcomen, Thomas: Set up the first pumping engine, forerunner of the steam engine, at Coventry, England.

Noah's Ark: Many forms, some with as many as 400 animals, not including Noah's family; mid-18th century.

—O—

optical toys: Stereoscopes, etc.

Ouija: A mystifying oracle game; invented by the Fuld brothers, Isaac and William, in the 1890s. U.S. government is still using it to make high-level decisions.

—P—

pace eggs: Hard-boiled egg with its shell colored or painted; English.

panoptique: Forerunner of the Magascope (opaque projector).

panorama toy: Commemorating the vast, all-round vista pictures perfected in Scotland; late 1700s. Some were claimed to be three miles long!

Pellerin: French toymaker; 1790s. His paper toys were . . .

penny toys: Sold for a penny in every country; 19th century. One cent, whether U.S., English, etc., was a lot of money in those days.

phenakistescope: Discs revolving on a spindle; each figure in a slightly different position. Peep-holer, 1830s.

picturegram: A paper picture rolled over a screen; invented by Edison. Accompanied by a Gramaphone record; 1929.

pigs-in-clover: The Shamrock, one of the oldest puzzle games.

pinching top: A spring wound about the top spindle that, when released by pinching, made the top spin.

plink-plunk: Music box action; from 1780s on. American versions were the best; 1850s.

polyopticon: Cheap type of magic lantern; American.

pot metal: Cheap dross; used to make inexpensive toys.

poupees: Dancing puppets controlled by wires and strings; Chinese in origin.

propeller: A three-wheeled form of velocipede; mid-1800s.

pull toy: Toy pulled by a string. A mobile was a pull toy that produced secondary effects, such as a figure or animal moving.

push toy (carpet): Toy pushed by hand on floor or road, etc.

—Q—

—R—

Reifentierens: German Noah's Ark animals; cleverly made from turned rings of wood, then sliced through to make each animal.

rotisserie: Victorian cookship; often made in child-size shapes.

rubber duck: Where did they come from? When? Joe Penner had a few!

—S—

sand toys: Sand powered the toy; teeter-tooters, etc.

Schoenhut: The greatest of them all! And still in business in Philadelphia.

scraps: A chromolithographic process that gave paper toys their shiny, bright colors; end of 19th century. Sold in sheets.

seaside toys: Miniature garden tools: used at seaside resorts; 1840s.

slinky: Large coiled spring, walked down steps; 1940s.

solitaire: "Tea for one"; a game of cards; a board with 37 holes.

spirit ships: Designed for a semi-religious purpose by early Egyptians.

spring-propelled top: Brought to Europe by Dutch seamen who had seen them used by natives in foreign countries.

steam toys: Heated boiler operated the engine.

stick horse: They go back to the early days of the Romans.

stencilling: Put on toys by using a cut-out; paint went over cuts.

still banks: Did nothing but hold the coins.

surprise box: A jack-in-the-box.

swinging weight toy: Heavy weight hanging beneath toy actuated it by swinging weight back and forth.

—T—

taquin (teaser): A square box divided into 16 compartments in which 15 numbered sliding pieces had to be arranged in a given order; French, late 1800s.

The Swiss Family Robinson: This book was first published in 1814!

tin: A soft, silver-white, metallic chemical element; malleable at ordinary temperatures.

toy theaters: Evolved from the earliest peep shows; a type of mobile cabinet carried by the peep show men; France and Italy, 17th century.

trolls: Danish dolls with grotesque faces and hair; designed by Thomas Dam.

trundling: The art of rolling one's hoop.

—U—

—V—

—W—

wheel toys: A toy that moves on wheels.

white mice: The name given to small rocking horses by English craftsmen; mid-1800s.

—X—

—Y—

yoyo: A momentum toy; up, down, up, down, etc.

—Z—

Zeppelin, Ferninand von: Launched his first rigid airship in 1900.

Zoetrope: Drawings are inserted in a revolving cylinder of cardboard and viewed through slits in the side as it rotated; made in U.S. by Milton Bradley Company, 1870s.

—A—

AIRPLANES

MARX AIRPLANE, tin mechanical windup, 1940s, **$35-$45.**

"BOLTS AND NUTS" TYPE, modern, hand-made, 1960s, **$4-$6.**

CAST IRON, single wing, early 1900s, **$20-$30.** U.S. ARMY, pot metal, Hubley, 1930s, 10" long, **$12-$17.** LUCKY BOY, cast iron, made by Dent, 1920s, **$8-$14.** MARX WORLD WAR II

FIGHTER, tin mechanical windup, **$6-$11.** MATCHBOX FIGHTER PLANES, 6 in set, 1940s, **$2-$4** each. KILLGORE "SEA GULL," propeller turns, 1930s, **$40-$45.**

POT METAL TYPES, 1930s, 2"-4" high, **$7-$12** each.

ALBUMS

SCRAP ALBUM, late 1800s, **$8-$12**.

"WILD FLOWERS, CATSKILLS," 1902, **$7-$11**.
"DOLLY'S FRIENDS," crude cutouts, **$4-$8**.

AMOS 'N ANDY

AMOS 'N ANDY CARD PARTY, A. M. Davis Company, 1930, **$1-$2** per card. FRESH AIR TAXICAB COMPANY OF AMERICA, INC., tin mechanical windup toy, 1930s, 8¼" long, **$285-$320**. MADAME QUEEN DOLL, plastic, **$45-$60**. ORIGINAL RADIO SCRIPT, "Amos' Wedding," 1935, **$95-$125**.

Amos Jones and Andrew H. Brown! Created and played on radio for more than 25 years by Charles Correll and Freeman Gosden. What a time when the King Fish, Ruby Taylor, Lightning, and Mrs. King Fish got together!

WALKING TOYS, tin mechanical windup, 1930s, **$155-$180** each.

ANDIRONS

HESSIAN SOLDIER, cast iron, one of a pair, mid-19th century, half size, **$170-$200** a pair.

During the Revolution, many Americans used the original Hessian andirons so they could "spit" at King George.

ANDY GUMP

Joe Patterson of the *Chicago Tribune* created Andy in 1917. Sid Smith did the actual drawing.

348 CAR, cast iron, Arcade, 1924. Three varieties: nickel-plated; more ornate; deluxe, 1924, **$85-$175.** CHESTER (Andy's son), in cast iron pony cart, 4½'' high, **$35-$45.** POT METAL ANDY-IN-CAR, Tootsietoy, 1932. Rare (the set). **$35-$45.**

AUTOS

"JETTA," tin friction, Germany, 1940s, **$10-$15.**

VW, cast iron, rubber tires, 1950s, **$25-$30.**

TIN LIZZIES, 1920s, **$125-$135** each.

CAR-WITH-TRAILER, pull toy, tin, 1930s, **$35-$45.**

14

"CASEY JONES," rider-type, metal, late 1930s, **$200-$250.**

"NAUGHTY BOY," tin mechanical windup, Lehmann, 1910, **$120-$140.**

LEHMANN'S AUTOBUS, miniature of real bus, it runs in circles (Don't we all?). Patented in U.S., May 1903. **$475-$575.**

LEHMANN TUT TUT, tin mechanical, man blows horn. Patented in U.S., September 1904. **$250-$275.** CAST IRON AUTO, Hubley, 1900s, **$8-$11.** FBI SQUAD CAR, tin friction, 1930s, **$25-$35.** MODEL T, cast iron, Arcade, late 1920s, 6'' long, **$65-$75.**

MERCEDES, tin mechanical windup, early 1900s, **$180-$225.**

ADVERTISEMENTS

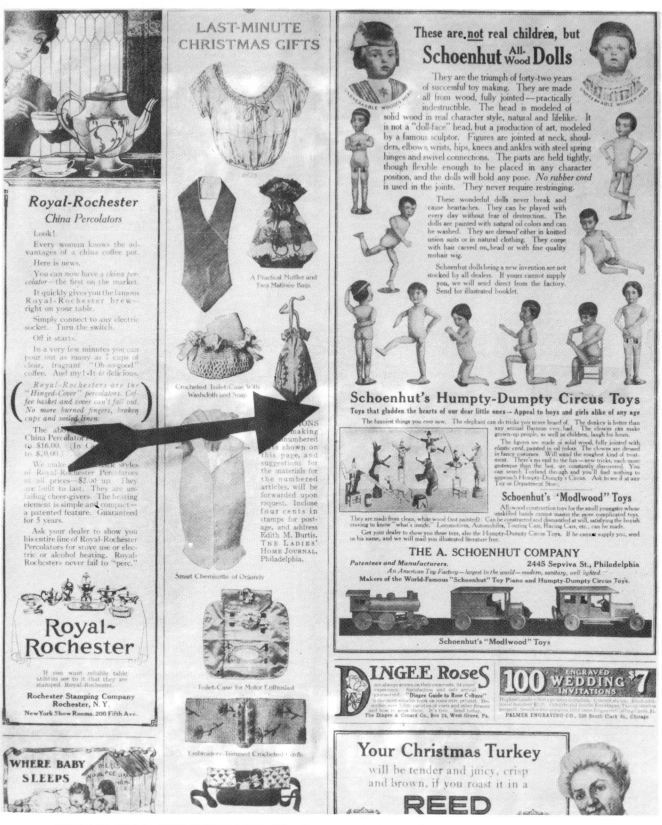

TYPICAL DOLL ADVERTISEMENT (illus.), 1914, **$2-$3.** EHRICH BROTHERS TOY PRICE LIST CATALOG, winter 1882, **$8-$14.** HUBLEY MANUFACTURING COMPANY "LANCASTER" IRON TOYS CATALOG, 1906, **$4-$7.** MARSHALL FIELD TOY CATALOG, 1894-1895, **$8-$14.**

—B—

BABY CARRIAGES

TIN TOLE (left), cloth top, 1920s, 2½'' long, **$12-$18**. TIN TOLE (right) cloth top, 1920s, 2'' long, **$12-$18**.

TWISTED WIRE BABY PRAM, dollhouse size, early 1900s, **$28-$38**.

METAL, folds down flat, wire wheels, 1920s, **$40-$50**. PEWTER, Victorian era, wheels turn, 8'' high, **$90-$110**. SPLIT REED, 1930s, 10'' high, **$30-$40**. GO-CART, hand-woven reed, Bessemer steel, 1900s, 22'' high, **$60-$80**. SLEEPER CART, with silk parasol, 1890s, 18'' high, **$195-$230**. GO-CART SLEEPER, with sateen parasol, wire wheels, 1900s, **$120-$140**.

SPLIT REED, 1920s, 24'' high, **$100-$125**.

BANK DESK

CARDBOARD, can actually be used, has safe in corner, etc., by Reed, 1882, 15" long, **$50-$60.**

BANKS, MECHANICAL

PUNCH AND JUDY, cast iron, **$300-$400.**

TWIRLING ELEPHANT-ON-DRUM, tin, 1930s, **$45-$60.**

STUMP SPEAKER, cast iron, late 1800s, **$475-$525.**

EAGLE BANK, 1892, **$450-$525.**
ORGAN BANK, 1891, **$265-$290.**
CAT AND DOG, 1893, **$265-$290.**
BICYCLE BANK, "Professor Pug Frog," etc., 1892, **$790-$840.**
PADDY AND HIS PIG, 1880s, **$500-$575.**

CLOWN, HARLEQUIN, AND COLUMBINE, J. & E. Stevens, 1906, **$650-$700.**

BASEBALL, cast iron, original box, made by J.&E. Stevens, Cromwell, Connecticut, 1840s, **$1,500-$1,700.**

THE INITIATING BANK—FIRST DEGREE, 1880s, **$1,400-$1,600.**

GOAT, FROG, AND OLD MAN, patented in 1880, **$900-$1,000.**

BANKS, STILL

NICKEL-PLATED BANK, combination lock, late 1800s, **$18-$24.**

PUBLIC TELEPHONE, 1930s, 10" high, **$35-$45.**

RABBIT, cast iron, 1920s, 5" high, **$40-$50**.

"SECURITY SAFE DEPOSIT," nickel-plated, combination lock, 1890s, **$18-$24.** "HOME SAVINGS" BANK, cast iron, 1890s, 6" high, **$13-$21.** SAFE-TYPE, cast iron, has key, 1890s, 3½" high, **$11-$18.** WATCHDOG SAFE, combination lock, 1890s, 6" high, **$18-$24.** "LANCASTER" HUBLEY BANK, No. 276, 1906, 4" high, **$8-$12.** "LANCASTER" HUBLEY BANK, No. 286, 1906, 5" high, **$16-$23.**

"HOME" BANK, tin, mid-1800s, 6" high, **$35-$40.**

BANKS, GLASS AND OTHER MATERIALS

LIBERTY BELL, tin screw base, late 1880s, 7" high, **$40-$45.** PIG, carnival glass, marigold color, 1920s, **$18-$25.** CERAMIC MOUSE, late 1800s, 4" long, **$25-$35.** CERAMIC PIGGY BANK, late 1800s, 4" long, **$23-$32.** CERAMIC ELEPHANT BANK, 1800s, 3½" high, **$25-$35.** CLAY (EARTHENWARE) BARREL, early 1900s, 4" high, **$8-$12.**

MINIATURE CAST IRON BANKS, 1930s, 4" and 5" high, **$20-$25** each.

BALANCE TOYS

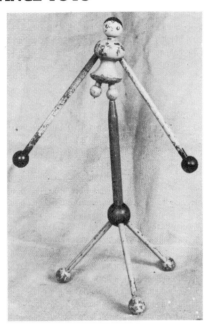

WOODEN "BALANCE" DOLL, two-piece, Germany, 1920s, **$35-$45.**

HO-KEE-PO-KEE-WIN-KEE-WUM MONKEY-ON-STRING, 1890s, **$80-$100.** CHARLIE CHAPLIN ON A TIGHTROPE, 1920s, **$285-$300.**

BASEBALLS

HAND-STITCHED, stuffed with straw, 1920s, **$5-$7** each.

OFFICIAL AMERICAN LEAGUE, signed "The Babe," 1920s, **$12-$14.** WORLD SERIES, Boston vs. New York, 15 signatures, 1920s, **$16-$18.**

BEST PARCHMENT RACKET, bound in red and gilt, complete with shuttlecock, 1882, **$45-$60.**

BEARS

 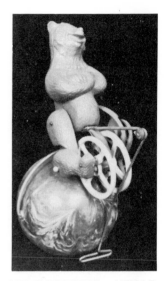

MINIATURE, "TED-DY," by Steiff, 1920s, 2½" high, **$45-$55.**

COMPOSITION "BEAR-ON-A-BALL," mechanical windup, 1940s, **$25-$35.**

DANCING BEAR, tin mechanical windup, 1930s, 8" high, **$30-$35.** "WRESTLING BEAR," tin mechanical windup, 1930s, **$30-$35.** BEAR PULL TOY, bell rings when pulled, 1920s, **$35-$40.**

BELL TOYS

HORSE-DRAWN "CHIME," cast iron, late 1800s, 6½" long, **$40-$50.**

DOG-AND-CAT-FIGHT, cast iron, 1890s, 9" long, **$40-$50.** DING DONG BELL, cast iron, 1890s, 5½" long, **$50-$55.** BELLRINGERS, cast iron and brass, 1892, 7" long, **$45-$55.** CHIME WITH HORSE, cast iron, 1894, 6½" long, **$45-$55.** GIRL-WITH-DOLL-ON-SLED, cast iron, Daisy, 1893, 9" long, **$55-$65.** JUMPING HORSE, MONKEY DRIVER, cast iron, 1892, 6" long, **$45-$55.**

BIRDS

MECHANICAL WINDUP, Germany, 1950s, **$18-$22**.

THE WALKING BIRD, pull toy, 1892, **$35-$45**.

BLISS TELEPHONE

TWO EARPHONES AND SPOOL OR WIRE, can be used in different rooms, obviously works on vibration process, 1882, **$120-$130**.

BLOCKS

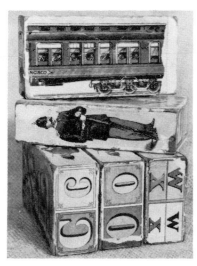

LITHOGRAPH-ON-CARDBOARD BLOCKS, alphabet, military, travel, mid-to-late 1800s, **$18-$25** set.

ABC BLOCKS, wood, 1920s, **$7-$9** complete set. PICTURE LEARNER BLOCKS, wood, late 1800s, **$14-$18**.

BOATS

TIN PULL TOY, late 1800s. The photographer is backward! **$250-$300**.

TIN BATTLESHIP, 1920s, **$35-$45**.

ORIENTAL "BOAT-IN-A-BOX," Japanese, 1930s, **$12-$20**.

WOODEN FIRE BOAT, painted, 1930s, **$18-$22**.

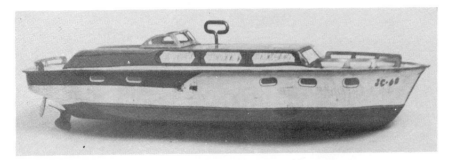

MOTOR BOAT, tin mechanical windup, 1920s, **$40-$60.**

MINIATURE PADDLE BOAT, cast iron, Wilkens Toy Company, Keene, New Hampshire, 1890s, 10½'' long, **$45-$55.**

TIN, a small candle made it move, Japan, 1940s, **$10-$15.**

STEAM-OPERATED BOAT, tin, 1900, **$125-$150.**

BATTLESHIP, an exact replica of America's first armed battleship, the U.S.S. New York, cardboard, **$100-$125.**

WOODEN BOAT, 1950s. The motor is a replica of a 1930s Evinrude outboard motor. It works! **$65-$75.**

TIN, a few cranks, Germany, 1940s, **$10-$15.** PAPIER-MACHE, German-made battleship, self-assembled, 1910,

BOUNCE TOY

"JIGGING NIGGER," wooden-jointed, early 1900s, **$45-$55.**

LITHOGRAPH-ON-WOOD DANCERS, wooden-jointed, 1890s, **$20-$30.** "TAP DANCER," tin, 1920s, 8" high, **$8-$12.** "DOLL AND PART-NER" (unbroken), composition, 1930s, **$30-$40.**

BREWERY

STEAM-OPERATED, brass-trimmed stationary engine, 1892, 12½" high. Unique! **$275-$325.**

BUCK ROGERS

ROCKET SHIPS, Tootsietoy, pot metal, pull toy, 1930s, 4"-5" long, "Venus Duo-Destroyer," "Battlecruiser," "Flash Blast Attack Ship," **$110-$125** each. POP GUNS, sheet metal, by Daisy, two types made, 1930s: "25th Century" pistol, 7½" and 9½" long, **$140-$160** each; "Disintegrator" pistol, 1930s, 10" long, **$125-$150.** "LIQUID HELIUM" WATER PISTOL, 1930s, **$85-$95.** ROCKET SHIP, tin mechanical windup, lithographed, Marx, 1930s, 12" long, **$120-$140.**

BUG

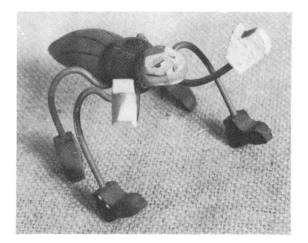

"BUG," obviously handmade so we call it a "primitive," 1920s variety, **$6-$8.**

BUS

CAST IRON BUS, Arcade Manufacturing Company, Freeport, Illinois, 1920s, **$120-$130.**

"OH BOY" BUS, No. 105, tin, 1920s, **$30-$40.**

GREYHOUND, cast iron, 1930s, 9" long, **$40-$50.** MARX ROYAL, lithographed, mechanical windup, 10" long, **$95-$120.** CAST IRON, salesman's sample (giveaway), 1930s, 6½" long, **$15-$25.** GREYHOUND, Tootsietoy, 1920s, 6" long, **$8-$13.** DOUBLEDECKER, friction toy, 1930s, 13" long, **$70-$85.** CAST IRON, rubber tires, Arcade, 1920s, **$28-$35.** DOUBLEDECKER, tin, friction, English, 1920s, **$45-$55.**

BUSTER BROWN

Dick Outcault, possibly riding on the "night-shirt of success"—his "The Yellow Kid" comic strip—created Buster and his dog Tige in 1902. Or recreated as the case may be.

BUSTER BROWN IN CART, 1900s, 7½" long, **$150-$175.**

—C—

CAMEL

TIN MECHANICAL WINDUP, late 1800s, **$135-$160.**

CANDLESTICKS

SOLID BRASS CANDLESTICKS, early 1900s, 2½" and 3" high, **$8-$12** each.

POT METAL TYPE, 1930s, 4" high, **$4-$5** pair. STERLING SILVER CANDELABRA, 1900s, 4½" high, **$150-$200** pair.

CANDY CONTAINERS

RAILROAD ENGINE, covered cab, clear, late 1800s, 6" long, **$80-$100.** PISTOL, clear, 7½" long, **$10-$14.**

AIRPLANE, tin wings, 1920s, **$30-$40.** GREY-HOUND BUS, 1930s, **$28-$35.** DONKEY PULL-ING BARREL, 1920s, **$30-$35.** LANTERN, wire bail handle, 1910s, 4" high, **$40-$48.** TELE-PHONE, tin receiver, 1930s, **$20-$28.** SCOTTIE DOGS, J. Crosetti Company **$40-$45** pair. DIRIGIBLE, "Shenandoah," 1930s, 8" long, **$38-$45.** SANTA CLAUS, red suit, otherwise clear, **$35-$45.** SUITCASE, tin closure, 1920s, 3¾" long, **$22-$32.** RABBIT-WITH-CARROT, 1930s, 4½" high, **$28-$35.**

CANNONS

"RAPID FIRE," cast iron, fired caps, early 1900s, **$35-$45.**

"SALUTING" CANNON, brass, French, 17th century, 30 " long, **$950-$1,100.**

CORK-FIRING-TYPE, pull back the lever..., 1910s, **$35-$45.**

"BIG BANG," carbide-type, 1930s, 3" barrel, **$22-$28.**

WOODEN CANNON, lithographed wheels, mid-1800s, **$35-$45.**

CAST IRON, painted, patented 1896, 5" long, **$30-$40.** BRASS BARREL, cast iron frame, by Ives, early 1900s, **$35-$45.** TOOTSIETOY, metal wheels, shoots, 1930s, **$26-$35.** POT METAL, spring-shot, 1920s, 6" long, **$20-$28.** TIN SPRING-SHOT, marked Hesse, 5½" long, **$14-$18.**

HANDMADE (primitive), 1940s, **$18-$25.**

CARRIAGES, HANSOMS, SURREYS, ETC.

BRAKE, iron, Hubley, 1906, 28" long, **$2,500-$3,500.**

CAST IRON, by Stanley Toys, U.S.A., 1900s, **$85-$95** as is, **$100-$125** complete.

HANSON, No. 661, iron, Hubley, late 1800s, 9¼" long, **$80-$90.** CAB, No. 662, iron, Hubley, late 1800s, 9¾" long, **$80-$90.** PONY PHAETON, cast iron, 1901, 11" long, **$120-$140.** MODEL LANDAU, cast iron, 1892, 16½" long, **$140-$160.** TALLY-HO, iron, 1893, 18" long, **$300-$375.** SUR-REY, cast iron, 1890s, 9½" long, **$80-$90.** BUCKBOARD, cast iron, Wilkens, 1895, 14" long, **$110-$120.** TANDEM TEAM, cast iron, Wilkens, 1895, 18½" long, **$110-$120.** BUGGY, No. 340, cast iron, Wilkens, 1895, 10½" long, **$90-$110.**

SINGLE-PAIR, cast iron, 1900s, **$175-$200.**

CARROUSELS (Merry-Go-Rounds)

MERRY-GO-ROUND, tin friction, Japan, 1940s, **$18-$25.**

CARROUSEL, tin mechanical, bisque-head dolls, 1880s, **$300-$350.**

"AIR-E-GO-ROUND," tin mechanical, Reeves, Milford, Connecticut, early 1900s, patent applied for, **$100-$125.**

MERRY-GO-ROUND, by Wolverine, 1920s, **$65-$85.** MERRY-GO-ROUND, clockwork toy, Althof, Bergman, New York City, late 1880s, **$400-$475.** CARROUSEL-WITH-SWINGS, clockwork toy, late 1800s, 12" high, **$165-$185.**

TIN-ON-IRON-ROD, pulley operated by rope, 1920s, **$100-$125.**

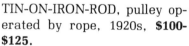

MERRY-GO-ROUND "RINGS," cast iron, 1894. You grabbed for a ring and got a free ride—if you didn't fall off and break your neck! **$10-$12** each.

TIN WINDUP, late 1800s, 9½" high, **$250-$300.**

CARTS

WOODEN CART, wool lamb, pull toy, 1900s, **$50-$70.**

WOODEN COAL CART, painted, late 1800s, **$25-$35.**

PONY CART, iron, Hubley, 1906, 10½'' long, **$65-$70.** ROAD CART, iron, Hubley, 1906, 8¼'' long, **$65-$70.** DUMP CART, iron, Hubley, 1906, 10½'' long, **$65-$70.** PONY CART, iron, Wilkens, 1895, 10½'' long, **$70-$85,** also with a "gentleman" driver, **$70-$85.** PONY CART, No. 141, iron, Wilkens, 1895, 10½'' long, **$70-$85.** ROAD CART, No. 440, iron, Wilkens, 1895, 8½'' long, **$70-$85.**

CASH REGISTERS

BENJAMIN FRANKLIN, tin, made by Kamkap, Inc., 1930s, **$45-$55.**

"PLAY STORE" TYPE, tin, 1920s, **$20-$30.**

CASTERS

COMPLETE SET IN POT METAL HOLDER, late 1800s, 4'' high, **$60-$80.**

28

CATS

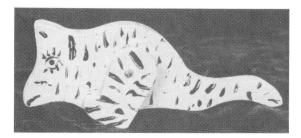

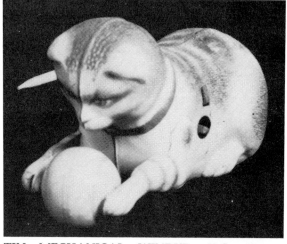

"CALICO CAT," wood, handmade, 1950s, **$8-$10.**

TIN MECHANICAL WINDUP, U.S. Zone, Germany, 1940s, **$8-$12.**

STEIFF CAT, mohair, stuffed, 1920s, **$45-$55.**

TIN MECHANICAL WINDUP, 1950s, **$35-$45.**

CHALKWARE "HEARTH" CAT, early 1900s, **$55-$65.**

The "Little Tramp" came to America in 1910. He left a few years later for Switzerland worth millions. That's the American way—ask any U.S. president!

CHARLIE CHAPLIN

CHARLIE CHAPLIN SQUEEZE TOY, German, 1920s, **$130-$170.** CHARLIE CHAPLIN DANCING TOY, tin, Germany, 1920s, **$95-$120.** BIKE RIDER, tin, lithographed, to balance on a string, 8" long, **$285-$300.** BELLRINGER, cast iron, painted, 1915-1918, **$160-$200.** "SHUFFLE" TOY, by Schuco, Germany, 8½" high, **$175-$250.** BOXER CHAMPION, Schuco, 1920s. Rare! **$475-$500.**

CHICKENS

"CHICKEN-IN-A-BASKET," tin mechanical, 1920s, 5½" high, **$18-$25.**

CHALKWARE CHICKEN-WITH-CHICKS, 1920s, **$25-$35.**

CHIMES

WOODEN "CHITTY CHIMES," lithograph on wood, eight buttons, each strikes a different note, late 1800s, **$75-$85.**

THE METALLOPHONE CHIMES, Ehrich Brothers, 1882, **$30-$35.**

CHECKERS

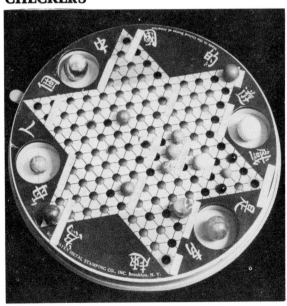

TIN CHINESE CHECKERS, clay balls, by Woodhaven Metal Stamping Company, Brooklyn, New York, 1920s, **$25-$35.**

WOODEN CHINESE CHECKERS, marbles, 1940s, **$8-$12.**

CHOPPERS

CAST IRON "BABY" CHOPPERS, 1900s, 5½" high, **$18-$22.** CAST IRON CHOPPERS, made in U.S., 1920s, **$8-$10.**

CAST IRON DAISY CHOPPERS, Hubley, late 1800s, **$18-$22.**

CLOWNS

CELLULOID/TIN CLOWN-AND-MONKEY, tin mechanical, 1930s, **$18-$22.**

CIRCUS

OVERLAND CIRCUS, animals in cages, iron, 1920, **$175-$225.**

BANK WAGON, iron, Hubley, 1920s, 30" long, **$150-$175.** CALLIOPE, cast iron, Hubley, 1920s, 16" long, **$150-$175,** ACROBAT WHEEL, cast iron, Wilkens, 1895, 9½" high, **$275-$350.** CLOWN VAN, cast iron, Hubley, 1895, 16½" long, **$275-$350.** REVOLVING MONKEY CAGE, iron, Hubley, 21½" long. Rare! **$450-$500.** GIRAFFE CAGE, iron, Hubley, 16½" long, **$120-$140.** GREAT AMERICAN ARENA AND MECHANICAL CIRCUS, late 1800s, **$250-$300.** JUMBO-ON-WHEELS, stuffed, 1882, 9" long, **$175-$200.** MECHANICAL ACROBATS, performing on bar, 1892, **$150-$200.** SCHOENHUT CIRCUS TOYS, see Schoenhut under "S."

TIN MECHANICAL, Japan, 1915, 9" high, **$100-$125.**

"WALKING-ON-HANDS" CLOWN, windup, by Chien, 1920s, **$28-$38.** "TWIRLING FLAG" CLOWN, tin, mechanical windup, Japan, 1930s, **$30-$35.** "CLOWN-ON-STICK," does tricks, late 1800s, **$75-$95.**

COACHES

"COACHMAN," mechanical windup, by Lehmann, early 1900s, **$145-$165.**

WOODEN "CINDERELLA" COACH, 1920s, **$25-$35.**

Remember when "Body by Fisher" gave college scholarships for the best designed cars in the 1930s? Whatever happened to them? Whatever happened to cars?

COMBS AND BRUSHES

CELLULOID COMB AND BRUSH, 1900s, **$7-$9** set.

COWS

"ANIMATED COW," the tail made it "moo," 1920s, **$25-$30.**

CALF, pull toy, "moos" as it goes, 1930s, 8½" high, **$20-$30.**

CRACKERJACK ITEMS

THE PRIZES, 1920s-1930s, **$2-$3** each.

CRANE

TIN MECHANICAL WINDUP, lithographed, 1930s, 11½" high, **$65-$75.**

CRAPSHOOTER

TIN WINDUP TOY, when in motion he throws dice onto table, 1930s, **$45-$60.**

CREEPING BABY

MADE OF IRON, painted and dressed, pulled by string, it moves along on hands and knees, 1882, **$375-$425.**

CUP AND BALL

PAINTED WOOD STICK AND BALL-ON-STRING, 1880s, **$20-$28.**

MINIATURE, Japanese, early 1900s, 1½" high, **$3-$6** set.

CUPS AND SAUCERS

MINIATURE, French, late 1800s. Cup, 1" diameter, **$2-$3;** saucer, 1½" diameter, **$2-$3.**

—D—

DEESTNCK SCHOOL

COMICAL SCHOOL FIGURES, cardboard, by Crandell, 1882, **$65-$75.**

DENNIS THE MENACE

TIN LITHOGRAPH, battery-operated, he plays xylophone, 1950s, **$20-$35.**

DIAMOND WAGON BLOCKS

BLACK WALNUT WAGON, filled with building blocks, 1882, **$150-$200.**

DICK TRACY

SQUAD CAR, tin mechanical windup, lithographed, Marx, 1949, 11" long, **$65-$75.** RIOT CAR, similar to squad car, **$65-$75.** B. O. PLENTY, tin mechanical windup, lithographed, Marx, late 1930s, **$50-$65.**

DINOSAURS

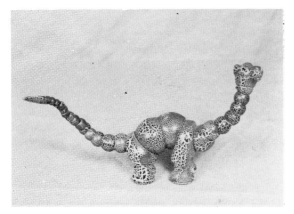

COMPOSITION, multi-jointed, 1930s, 13'' long, **$8-$12.**

Remember when Sinclair used "Dinny" as a publicity stunt?

DOGS

POT METAL, mid-1900s, **$8-$12.**

PENNSYLVANIA CHALKWARE, late 1800s, **$65-$75.**

WOOD-CARVED, mid-1800s, 22'' long, **$45-$55.**

TIN DOG-IN-HOUSE, chases cat, mechanical, 1930s, **$18-$25.** "SANDY," composition, 1930s, **$38-$48.** STUFFED BEAGLE, mohair-covered, Steiff, 1920s, **$45-$60.** TIN, mechanical wind-up, sits up, 1930s, **$30-$40.**

DOLLS

RUSSIAN "NEST" DOLLS, papier-mache, eight in set, early 1900s, **$70-$90.**

Love dolls? Buy the *Wallace-Homestead Price Guide to Dolls.* I know, I wrote it!

TIN MECHANICAL, French, 1900s, **$100-$120.**

POT METAL DOLL, 1920s, 6'' high, **$35-$45.**

WOOD-AND-PIPESTEM-CLEANER DOLL,
primitive, 1950s, **$8-$10.**

DOLLHOUSES

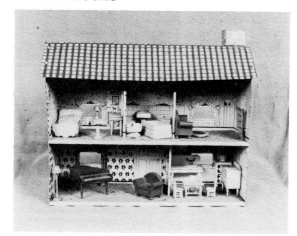

TIN DOLLHOUSE, wooden furniture 1930.
Dollhouse, **$25-$35;** wooden furniture, **$12-$18**
each.

DOMINOES

IVORY SET, in wooden box, early 1900s, **$25-$35**.

"DOMINOES," by Halsam, 1930s, **$10-$15**.

DOORSTOPS

CAST IRON DOORSTOPS, for child's door, late 1800s, **$55-$65** each.

DREDGE AND CONVEYOR

STEAM-OPERATED, stationary engine, 1892, 9" high, **$175-$200**.

DRUMS

TIN DRUM WITH WOODEN STICKS, 1940s, **$18-$22**.

LITHOGRAPH-DECORATED DRUM, with sticks, early 1900s, **$18-$22**.

DUMBBELLS

WOODEN, maple 1-pound size, early 1900s, **$5-$7**.

—E—

ELECTRIC MOTORS

REX DYNAMO MOTOR, with grinder and jigsaw, early 1900s, **$45-$55** complete.

FORGE, complete with 151 motor and battery, 1892, **$65-$80.** DREDGE AND CONVEYOR, with 151 motor and battery, 1892, **$75-$90.** "MERRY-GO-ROUND," with 151 motor and battery, 1892, **$160-$175.**

—F—

FIREARMS

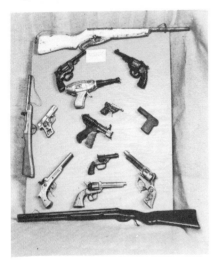

EXAMPLES OF CAP PISTOLS, WATER PISTOLS, PISTOLS THAT USED A ROLL OF PAPER, POPGUNS, AIRGUNS. Cap pistols first appeared during the 1876 Centennial in Philadelphia. The ages of examples here vary from late 1800s to 1940s. **$2.50-$300.**

FIRE ENGINES

CAST IRON, driver missing, 1920s, **$200-$250.**

CAST IRON, Kenton Toys, Kenton, Ohio, late 1920s, **$150-$175.**

CAST IRON HOSE REEL, two horses, Hubley-tpe, 1900s, 20" long, **$250-$275.**

WOODEN, hand-carved, two horses, 1900s, 10½" long, **$100-$125.**

TIN HOOK-AND-LADDER (wooden ladders), late 1800s, **$125-$150.**

TOOTSIETOY, sprayer, 1930s, 3" long, **$25-$35.** AUTO FIRE ENGINE, No. 460, Hubley, 1900s, 7" long, **$65-$75.** POT METAL FIRE TRUCK, 1930s, **$18-$22.** HOSE WAGON, cast iron, two horses, late 1800s, **$195-$250.** FIRE CHIEF'S CAR, friction toy, Japan, 1920s, 11½" long, **$28-$38.** FIRE CHIEF'S CAR, painted tin, mechanical windup, Chien, 1920s, **$95-$135.** FIRE ENGINE, cast iron, mechanical windup, 1890s, 19" long, **$325-$400.** AUTO WATER TOWER, No. 488, cast iron, Hubley, 1900s, 31" long, **$175-$200.** AUTO PATROL, No. 444, cast iron, Hubley, 1900s, 15" long, **$150-$190.** AUTO HOOK-AND-LADDER, No. 555, iron, Hubley, 1900s, 29" long, **$275-$300.** REEL PATROL, No. 442, iron, Hubley, 1900s, 15¾" long, **$150-$200.**

FLAGS

CLOTH FLAGS, came in packs of cigarettes, 1920s, **$3-$5** each.

FLAMINGO

CRUDE, handmade primitive, 1920s. Many people couldn't afford the luxury of buying toys in those days. **$3-$5.**

FORGE

STEAM-OPERATED, stationary engine, has whistle steam pipe, 1892, 10" high, **$175-$200.**

FORTRESSES

COMPOSITION/WOOD, folds up, 1930s, 24" long, **$10-$12.**

WOODEN BLOCK-TYPE, blocks came in large chest, 1920s, **$200-$250.** ERECTOR SET-TYPE, metal, in cardboard box, 1920s, **$85-$95.**

FOUNTAIN

STEAM-OPERATED FOUNTAIN, stationary brass-finished engine, 1892, 9" high, **$175-$200.**

FURNITURE

WALNUT VICTORIAN BED, hinged head and foot, 1850s, 6" long, **$75-$85.**

OAK KITCHEN CABINET, late 1800s, 5" high, **$25-$35;** ironston pieces, **$3-$5** each; glass candlesticks, **$5-$7** pair.

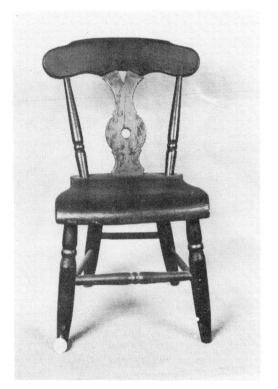

PLANK BOTTOM PERIOD CHAIR, mid-19th century, **$150-$175.**

WOODEN CHAIR, reed bottom, Mexico, modern, **$3-$5.**

WICKER CHAIRS, 1920s, **$4-$8** set.

SPOKEBACK CHAIR, Kentucky, 1790s, 22'' high, **$150-$175.**

MAHOGANY CHILD'S CHAIR, 1800s, 25'' high, **$800-$900.**

LIVING ROOM SUITE, wood, painted blue, six pieces, 1920, **$35-$40** set. DINING ROOM SUITE, wood, seven pieces, 1920, **$40-$45** set. BUREAU, decorated in three colors, brass drawer pulls, 1880s, 23'' high, **$40-$50.**

—G—

GALLOPING HORSE AND BUGGY

TIN MECHANICAL CLOCKWORK, horse gallops, driver plies whip, 1882, 18'' long, **$175-$225**.

GARAGES

TIN, lithographed, holds two cars, 1930s, 7'' high, **$35-$45**; with two windup cars, **$120-$130**. LITHOGRAPHED PAPER ON WOOD, two horse-drawn wagons, top is removeable, 1890s, 10'' high, **$200-$225**.

GEM SOLITAIRE

DELIGHTFUL PASTIME FOR A SINGLE PLAYER, pins and board, in box, 1882, 6'' long, **$40-$45**.

GOLLIWOGS

CYCLING GOLLIWOG, stuffed doll, English, 1930s, 9'' high, **$85-$95**. PORCELAIN CHILD'S MUG, green, Germany, 1920s, 2½'' high, **$35-$40**.

GRASSHOPPERS

HAND-CARVED, wooden, 1960s, **$8-$12**.

GROCERY STORE

COMPLETE WITH COUNTER, SCALES, cardboard, drawers open and close, shelves stocked with trade goods, 1880s, 11'' long, **$95-$125**.

GYROSCROPES

POT METAL, complete with instructions, 1930s, **$12-$18**.

BRASS RINGED, iron pedestal included, 1880s, **$35-$45**.

Charles Darrow, inventor of "Monoply," developed the game for his own amusement. When Parker Brothers turned it down, Darrow had 5,000 sets made and sold them to Wanamakers, a large department store in Philadelphia. In 1935, Parker Brothers offered Darrow a royalty contract. Since then, Parker Brothers has sold more than 70 million sets, making "Monopoly" the world's most popular board game.—Photo courtesy Parker Bros.

GAMES

WOODEN "MARBLE" GAME, 1890s, **$15-$18.**

"THE MANSION OF HAPPINESS," Parker Brothers, 1885, **$15-$18.** —Photo courtesy Parker Bros.

43

"WATERLOO," Parker Brothers, Salem, Massachusetts, 1895,
$15-$18. —Photo courtesy Parker Bros.

"A GAME OF CHRISTIAN ENDEAVOR," Parker, 1890, **$14-$16.** —Photo courtesy Parker Bros.

"THE RACE FOR THE CUP," Parker, 1869-1903, **$14-$16.**—Photo courtesy Parker Bros.

"CHIVALRY," by George S. Parker, Salem, Massachusetts, 1887, **$16-$18.**
—Photo courtesy Parker Bros.

"THE GAME OF BANKING," first Parker game, 1883, **$16-$18.** —Photo courtesy Parker Bros.

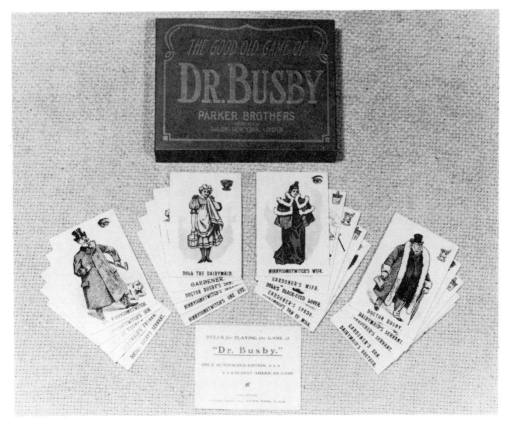

"DR. BUSBY," Parker, 1915-1934, **$15-$18.** —Photo courtesy Parker Bros.

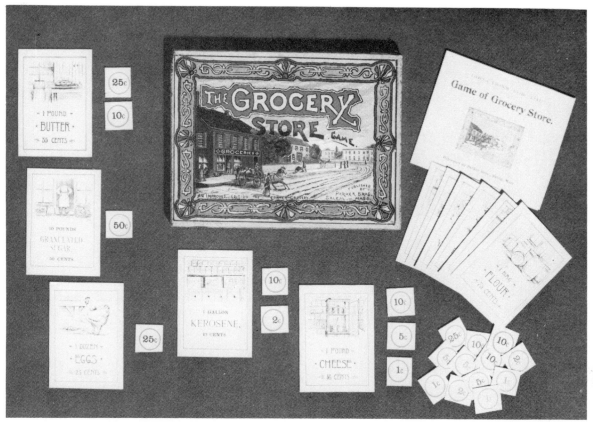

"THE GROCERY STORE," Parker Brothers, 1887, **$18-$30.**—Photo courtesy Parker Bros.

"BACKGAMMON," ivory pieces in ebony box, 1890s, **$165-$190.** FOOTBALL GAME, pinball-type, on legs, 1920s, 38" high, **$195-$250.**

"PARCHEESI," original pieces, dice, board, 1920s, **$15-$19.** "ROOK," complete, 1920s, **$12-$18.**

—H—

HAM AND SAM

TIN MECHANICAL WINDUP, by Strauss, 1920s, **$200-$225.**

HATCHETS

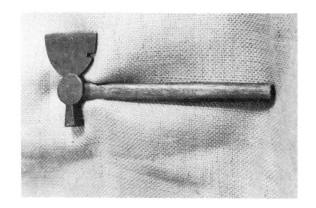

Hand-forged, 1900s, 11" long, **$12-$18.**

HEN AND CHICKEN

"HEN-AND-CHICKEN" GAME, bouncing ball-on-string made figures "peck" on board, Germany, 1900s, **$18-$22.**

HENRY

HENRY THE ACROBAT, tin mechanical wind-up, 1930s, **$100-$130.** HENRY RUNNING AWAY, tin mechanical windup, 1930s, **$150-$175.** HENRY ON ELEPHANT'S TRUNK, tin mechanical windup, 1930s, **$130-$160.**

HOPALONG CASSIDY

TIN MECHANICAL WINDUP, lithographed, Marx, 1950s, 11" long, **$80-$100.** TEN-GALLON HAT, original band, 1950s, **$25-$35.** "OFFICIAL" SIX-GUN, 1950s, **$22-$30.** COMIC BOOK, early 1950s, **$8-$10** each.

HORSES

HORSE-IN-HOOP, tin, horse trots, Merriam Manufacturing Company, Durham, Connecticut, 1870s. Various sizes, 4½" to 12" in diameter. **$85-$95.**

TRICYCLE, tin, rubber hand grips and pedals, 1920s, **$150-$175.**

ROCKING HORSE, wooden, spring-type, mohair-covered, 1900s, **$450-$500.**

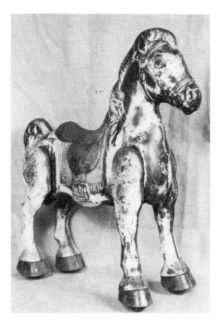

ENGLISH "RIDER," moves as you bounce up and down, 1950s, 25'' high, **$75-$85**.

COMPOSITION, with leather harness, 1900s, **$75-$90**.

ROCKING HORSE, wooden, real hair tail, late 1800s, **$450-$500**.

COMPOSITION PULL TOY, wooden wheels, Germany, 1950s, **$14-$19**. MECHANICAL WINDUP, tin, lithographed, 1920s, **$65-$75**. TIN MECHANICAL WINDUP, cowboy goes up and down, 1930s, **$40-$50**. WOODEN PULL TOY, lithographed, 1920s, **$45-$55**.

HUMPTY-DUMPTY PANTOMIME

LARGE, SHOWY TOY, the clown goes through many of his tricks, takes 10 minutes to do everything. This toy cost $12 in 1882! **$375-$400**.

HURDY-GURDY

WOODEN "HURDY-GURDY," played a musical disc, late 1800s, **$180-$240**; extra discs, **$25** each.

Who can ever forget the organ grinder and his trained monkey on a leash that tipped its hat when you dropped money in its tin cup?

—I—

INDIANS

TIN MECHANICAL WINDUP, 1940s, **$40-$50.**

LEAD INDIANS, set of 24, mounted, walking, etc., 1930s, **$50-$65** set. LEAD INDIANS, set of 12, English, 1920s, **$22-$32.** NAVAJO BLANKET, child-size, handwoven, 1930s, **$65-$80.** CHILD'S MOCCASINS, buckskin, "silver" buttons, 1930s, **$20-$30** pair. CHILD'S BOW AND ARROW, six arrows in set, 1920s, **$30-$40.** CHILD'S CHIEF BONNET, eagle feathers, felt trim, 1920s, **$180-$220.**

IRONS

MINIATURE, detachable handle, late 1800s, 2" long, **$28-$38.**

MINIATURE IRONING BOARD, 1930s, 11" high, **$6-$8.** MINIATURE FLAT IRON, 1900s, **$18-$22.**

SWAN-SHAPED FLAT IRON, 1900s, 2½" long, **$20-$25.** Often called "sadirons," probably because you were when it came time to iron.

—J—

JACK IN THE BOX

CARDBOARD, painted head-on-spring, latch cover on box, 1882, **$60-$70.** BUGABOO MAN, 1882, **$65-$75.**

JOE PALOOKA

I remember the "Joe Palooka" Bar and Grill in Wilkes-Barre, Pennsylvania—1940s. A great joint! So was Kitty's—same town. Oh, well! Ham Fisher created Joe and friends.

HUMPHREY MOBILE, lithographed sheet metal, 1930s, 9" long, **$80-$90.** LITTLE MAX, on handmade scooter, 1930s, 7" long, **$85-$90.**

JOE PENNER

JOE PENNER, tin mechanical windup, lithographed, Marx, 1930s, 8" high, **$250-$300.** PENNER RIDING ON A DUCK, rocker toy, cardboard, 1930s, **$70-$85.**

—K—

KATZENJAMMER KIDS

Toys based on Rudy Dirk's comic strip, 1897. Hans and Fritz kept Mama and der Captain busy.

"SIGHT-SEEING AUTO," cast iron, Kenton, 1911, **$125-$140.** DONKEY CART, tin mechanical windup, 1900s, **$175-$190.**

KID SAMPSON

TIN MECHANICAL WINDUP, "B & R" trademark, patented 1921, **$75-$85.**

KINORA

KINORA, similar in size to a small table stereoscope, presents to the eye photographic views in motion, much like a flicker box, English, 1890s, **$125-$150.**

KITCHENWARE

TIN, 1900s, **$6-$9** each.

GRANITEWARE, 1900s, **$8-$10** each.

TIN, 1900s, **$6-$9** each.

CAST IRON/TIN, 1900s, **$6-$9** each.

EARLY ALUMINUM PIECES, 1930s, 2''-2½'', **$2-$3** each.

MEXICAN, textile fiber, 1940s, 24' long, **$12-$16**; 8' long, **$8-$10**.

WOVEN HORSE HAIR, 1930s, 24' long, **$35-$50**. Also known as riatas and lasoos.

L'IL ABNER BAND

TIN MECHANICAL WINDUP, complete with instruction sheet, Unique Manufacturing Company, Newark, New Jersey, 1945, **$225-$250**.

—L—

LAMPS

MINIATURE, glass, tin handle, late 1800s, 2½''high, **$6-$8**.

LIONS

LARIATS

STUFFED ''RIDING'' TYPE, on wheels, 1900s, 22'' high, **$85-$100**.

STUFFED, mohair-covered, late 1800s, 18'' high, **$95-$120**. WOODEN, hand-carved, 1900s, 8'' long, **$80-$95**. STUFFED, mohair-covered, Schwartz, 1950s, 6' high, **$150-$200**.

WOODEN HORSE, pull toy, real hair in tail and mane, 1900s, 16" high, **$100-$125**.

THE EMERALD CITY OF OZ (illus.), **$15-$18**. THE LOST PRINCESS OF OZ (illus.), **$15-$18**. THE LAND OF OZ, **$25-$35**. OZMA OF OZ, **$25-$35**. DOROTHY AND THE WIZARD OF OZ, **$45-$55**. THE PATCHWORK GIRL OF OZ, **$25-$35**. THE SCARECROW OF OZ, **$25-$35**. Written by L. Frank Baum, illustrated by John R. Neill, and published by Reilly and Britton Company, Chicago, Illinois, in 1910. From the beginning, Oz books were a hit with young and old alike. Then Judy Garland tripped the light fantastic "down the yellow brick road" with Jack Haley (the Tin Man), Bert Lahr (the Cowardly Lion), Ray Bolger (the Scarecrow), Frank Morgan (the Wizard of Oz), and a host of others.

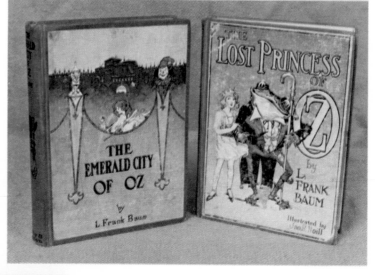

EMPIRE STOVE, Metalware Corp., Two Rivers, Wisconsin. Made in the 1920s, it actually worked and was a salesman's sample. 110 volts, 300 watts, 16" high, **$125-$150**.

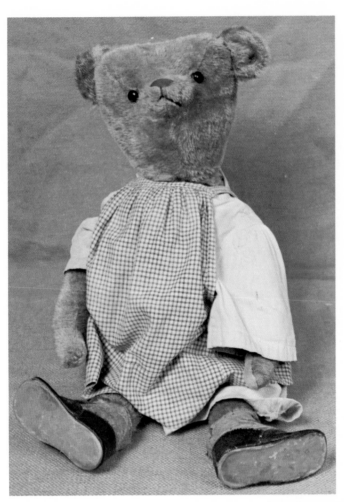

"TEDDY" BEAR, stuffed mohair with leather shoes, originally had a button in each ear, 1906. Rare. **$75-$85.**

CHILD'S CHINA CABINET, maple, turn of the century, 6" high, **$45-$65.** Items in cabinet include Bristol glass, Lattacino stemmed goblets, pottery/porcelain, **$1-$2** each and up.

CHILD'S TEA SERVICE, early 1900s. All pieces marked "Mexico." The McKinley Act of 1904 required imports to be marked as to country of origin. **$12-$18** complete.

ROYAL BAYREUTH CHILD'S BOWL AND PITCHER, 1900s. Bowl, **$20-$25**; pitcher, **$18-$25**.

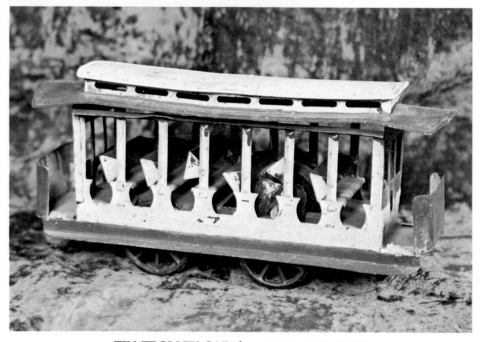

TIN TROLLEY CAR, late 1800s, **$200-$250**.

WOODEN PULL TOYS, early 1900s. Fur-covered (left),
4½" high, **$65-$75;** mohair-covered (right), 3⅔" high,
$45-$55.

STUFFED TIGERS, 1940s. Steiff tiger
(left), **$6-$8;** "Designed by Character"
tiger (right), **$15-$18.**

STUFFED CAMEL, by Steiff, 1960s,
$6-$8. STUFFED TURTLE, Germany,
1960s, **$5-$7.**

"MAMMOTH" STORY BLOCKS, litho-
graphs over wood, 10 to a set, patented
June 28, 1881. Possibly Crandell.
$85-$95 set.

MINIATURE CELLULOID WALT DISNEY CHARACTERS, in original boxes, 1940s, figures ¾'' high. Rare. **$8-$12** each. MICKEY MOUSE, 3'' high, **$25-$35.**

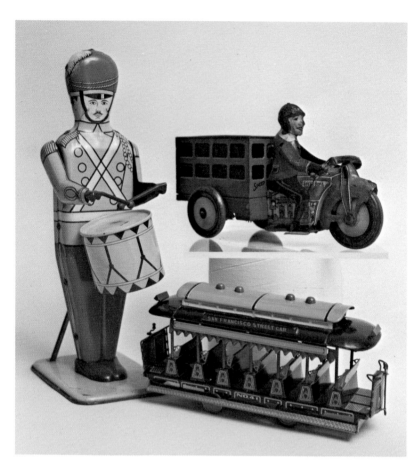

SOLDIER, tin mechanical windup, 1910, **$95-$110**. SPEEDBOY 4, tin mechanical windup, 1920s, **$60-$75**. SAN FRANCISCO STREET CAR, No. 41, tin, 1900s, **$125-$140**.

WOODEN CANNON, 1900s, **$25-$35**. WOODEN PULL TOY, early 1900s, **$125-$140**. WOODEN FIGURE-ON-HORSE, clockwork mechanism, 1900s, **$65-$80**.

CAST IRON PULL TOY, 1900s, **$85-$110**. CAST IRON FIRE ENGINE, rubber tires, 1920s, **$90-$120** complete.

LEHMANN TUT TUT, tin mechanical, driver blows horn, etc., patented in U.S., September 1904, **$85-$100**. OVERLAND CIRCUS WAGON, cast iron, 1900s, similar to Hubley's "Lancaster" line, **$130-$145** complete. OVERLAND CIRCUS BANDWAGON, cast iron, 1900s, 30" long, **$185-$220** complete.

LONE RANGER

TIN MECHANICAL WINDUP, lithographed, Silver rears up, Marx, 1938, **$95-$110**.

—M—

MAGIC LANTERNS

TIN, barrel of lantern sits directly on lamp, 1890s, 16'' high, **$25-$35**.

BRASS/TIN, 10¾'' high, **$25-$35**. COMPLETE MAGIC LANTERN KIT, tickets, brass lantern, original box with 12 slides, late 1800s, **$75-$90**. SLIDES FOR MAGIC LANTERNS, **$2-$4** each. Kaleidoscopes operated on a mirror basis, triangle effect, etc.

MAIL TRUCKS, WAGONS

TIN MECHANICAL WINDUP, 1920s, **$45-$60**.

CAST IRON PULL TOY, late 1800s, **$80-$95**.
WOODEN, lithographed, 1920s, **$35-$40**.

MAN AT SAW

TIN, cam connected to saw animated the man, clockwork mechanism, 1930s, **$25-$35** each.

MARBLES

ASSORTMENT OF CLAY TYPE, (illus.) late 1880s, **$1-$2** each.

AGATE TYPE, late 1800s, **$6-$7** each. SUL-PHIDE, Goat, **$25-$35;** Angel, **$35-$45;** Fish (two passing), **$70-$80;** Girl (kneeling), **$35-$50;** Elephant, **$25-$35.**

MATCHBOX TOYS

DOLLS BLOCKS/PHOTOS, original box, late 1800s, **$12-$16** set.

SMALLEST TRAIN, original box, early 1900s, **$9-$17** set.

SMALLEST KITCHEN, original box, early 1900s, **$7-$15.**

SAND/GRAVEL TRUCK, 1913 MERCER, **$8-$10** each.

SPORTS CARS, **$8-$10** each.

TOURING, BUGATTI, MODEL T, **$7-$9** each.

MECHANICAL ATTACHMENTS FOR TOY STEAM ENGINES

THE OLD MILL, THE SMOKER, THE ORGAN GRINDER, VILLAGE PUMP, ROMEO AND JULIET, all 1892, all 6'' x 6'', **$120-$140** each.

MERRY MAKERS

TIN MECHANICAL WINDUP, by Marx, 1920s, **$210-$250**.

MICKEY MOUSE AND FRIENDS

MICKEY MOUSE CIRCUS TRAIN, tin mechanical windup, lithographed, Lionel, 1935. Contents: cardboard tent, composition Mickey, several other characters and items, **$800-$900**. MICKEY MOUSE TRAIN, Marx, 1940s, **$95-$110**. MICKEY MOUSE HANDCARS, four made by Lionel in 1935, 7"-9" long, **$300-$350** each. DONALD DUCK REGISTER BANK, **$60-$70**. DONALD DUCK HANDCAR, **$350-$400**. COMPOSITION MICKEY MOUSE TREASURE CHEST BANK, **$40-$50**. MICKEY MOUSE, wooden, jointed, 1920s, 6" high, **$75-$95**. Lithographed tin and sheet metal were the most common materials used.

MILITARY FIGURES

CAST IRON SOLDIERS, 1920s, **$7-$9** each. TRENCH BAG, **$2-$3**.

FRICTION TOY SOLDIER, 1920s, **$35-$45**.

MINIATURE SUIT OF ARMOR, handmade, Germany, early 1800s, 32" high, **$800-$875**.

MARINE, ARMY, NURSE CORPS, SAILOR, 1920s, **$7-$9** each.

WOODEN KNIGHT, hand-carved, European, 19th century, **$45-$65.**

MINIATURE DRESDEN SOL-DIERS, early 1800s, 2″ high, **$75-$85** each.

MILK WAGON

TIN MECHANICAL WINDUP, 1930s, **$60-$90.**

MONKEYS

FELT-COVERED TIN MONKEY, danced when tapped on roof, **$85-$95.**

TIN MECHANICAL WINDUP, mohair coat, Japan, 1920s, **$10-$15.**

TIN MECHANICAL WINDUP, dressed as Uncle Sam, 1930s, **$35-$50.**

IVORY, hand-painted, late 1800s. "See no, hear no . . ." **$15-$18.**

MOON MULLINS (AND KAYO)

RAILROAD HANDCAR, ran on tracks, Marx, 1930s, regular model, **$175-$190;** deluxe model, **$300-$325.** UNCLE WILLY AND MAMIE, in boat, tootsietoy, 1932, **$50-$60.** MOON IN POLICE PATROL, tootsietoy, 1932, **$50-$60.**

MOTORCYCLES

CAST IRON, 1920s, 6'' long, **$10-$15.**

CAST IRON, 1920s, 5½'' long, **$15-$25.**

CAST IRON, rubber wheels, Hubley, 1920s, 9¾'' long, **$15-$25.**

CAST IRON, both Hubley, 1900s, **$18-$28.**

MOUNT VERNON

WOOD/CARDBOARD, home and burial place of George Washington, 1890s, 28" wide, **$350-$400.**

MOXIE

TIN MECHANICAL WINDUP, 1920s. Advertisement for one of the world's worst tasting soft drinks! **$200-$225.**

MUSICAL

"ORIGINAL EMMET RICHTER HARMONICA," tin/wood, 1920s, **$3-$5.**

BRASS BAND BELL HARMONICA, early 1900s, **$25-$35.** IMITATION MAHOGANY ACCORDIAN, 1900s, 10¼ high, **$35-$45.** M. HOHENE'S "NEWEST AND BEST" HARMONICA, 10 double holes, 1900s, **$6-$9.** JEW'S HARP, early 1900s, 2¼"-4¼" frame, **$4-$9** each.

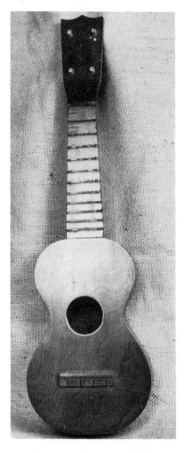

UKE, four-string, 1920s, 13½" long, **$25-$35.**

MUTT AND JEFF

Bud Fisher, by 1908, had these two characters in the newspaper comic strip.

SHEET STEEL MECHANICAL MUTT AND JEFF, mechanical windup, lithographed, German, 1920s, **$90-$100.**

STILL BANK, 1920s, **$45-$70.**

PLASTER FIGURES, felt clothes, Swiss, 1940s, 8" and 6½" high, **$85-$95** each.

—N—

NINEPINS

HARDWOOD PINS AND BALLS, painted, in square wooden box, 1882, **$85-$90.**

"ARTILLARY TENPINS," similar to hardwood pins and balls, large wooden cannon, 18" long, shot rubber ball at set of tenpins, 1882, **$150-$175.**

NOAH'S ARKS

WOODEN PULL/PUSH (carpet) TOY, with painted animals, 1920s, **$18-$22** set.

WOODEN PULL TOY, lithographed paper on wood, early 1900s, **$40-$50**.

WOODEN ARK ANIMALS, hand-carved, late 1800s, **$3-$5** each.

WOODEN CARVED ARK AND FIGURES, 1900s, **$9-$15**.

NOVELTIES, JOKES

PLATE LIFTERS, rubber ball under plate, squeeze, etc., 1920s, **$2-$5.** SPRINGING CIGARETTES, open case, out they fly, 1920s, **$2-$3.** FEARSOME DAGGER, made of rubber, 1920s, 8" long, **$8-$9.** SMALLEST MOUTH ORGAN IN THE WORLD, 1920s, 1¼" long, **$12-$16.**

—O—

—P—

PAILS

SAND PAIL, tin, 1950s, **$4-$6.**

LITHOGRAPH ON TIN, wood handle, 1920s, **$8-$12.**

WOODEN PAIL, steel-banded, 1900s, **$8-$12.** LITHOGRAPH ON TIN, alphabet, Chien, 1920s, **$8-$12.**

PAINT SETS

HOWDY DOODY, water colors, 1950s, **$8-$10.** MICKEY MOUSE, water colors, 1930s, **$60-$70.** ALICE IN WONDERLAND, water colors, 1920s, **$40-$50.** SHIRLEY TEMPLE, water colors, 1930s, **$35-$45.**

PAN, DUST

TIN (tole), late 1800s, **$8-$12.** RUSH BROOM, 1920s, **$3-$4.**

PHONOGRAPHS

PIANOS

BABY GRAND, tin, Schoenhut, 1900s, **$85-$125.**

MINIATURE "BABY CABINET," windup type, made by Garford Manufacturing Company, Elyria, Ohio, 1900s, **$100-$125.** RECORDS, for this phonograph, **$6-$8** each.

PHOTOGRAPHS

WOODEN SCHOENHUT, with stool, note candle holders, 1900s, **$125-$150** both.

BOY WITH TRICYCLE, in walnut/gold frame, late 1800s, **$40-$45.**

MINIATURE "PLAYER," "Piano Lodeon,"
Chien, London, England, and U.S., 1960,
$80-$90. "PLAYER" ROLLS, **$1-$2** each.

PICTUREGRAM

PANORAMIC PICTURES, syncronized with
gramophone records, made by Thomas Edison
in 1929, windup toy, locking case, **$275-$300.**

PILE DRIVER

STEAM-OPERATED, A. Buckman, Brooklyn,
New York, 1890s, **$90-$125.**

PINBALL MACHINES

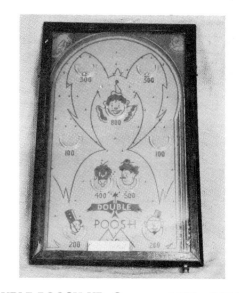

WOODEN SCHOENHUT, six-key, patented
September 18, 1900, **$55-$75.**

WOODEN UPRIGHT, Japan, 1930s, **$30-$40.**

DOUBLE POOSH-UP, German, 1930s, **$45-$65.**

PIP SQUEAKS

PENNSYLVANIA DUTCH, papier-mache, they squeaked when squeezed, early 1800s, **$35-$50** if working.

PLATES

CERAMIC BUSTER BROWN, Germany, 1900s, 2½" in diameter, **$15-$18.**

CERAMIC ALPHABET, Germany, late 1800s, 2½" in diameter, **$40-$50.**

CERAMIC BROWNIES, Palmer Cox, 1896, **$35-$45.** CERAMIC FRANKLIN PROVERBS (Meakin), **$40-$50.** GLASS ELEPHANT CENTER, 6", **$35-$45.** GLASS HEN AND CHICKS, **$25-$30.** GLASS LITTLE BO PEEP, **$30-$40.** PEWTER PIGS-IN-PEN, **$60-$70.** PEWTER

TOWER OF LONDON, dated 1805, **$80-$90.** TIN HI DIDDLE DIDDLE, **$35-$45.** TIN JUMBO, **$35-$45.** TIN MARY HAD A LITTLE LAMB, **$25-$35.** TIN WHO KILLED COCK ROBIN?, **$25-$35.**

PLAYING CARDS

COPIES OF EARLY PLAYING CARDS, **$8-$10** each. Originals would bring double.

POOL PLAYER

TIN MECHANICAL WINDUP, player shoots steel balls, 1920s, **$65-$75.**

POOR OLD JOE

WOODEN PULL TOY, wool-covered, donkey nods head, 1882, 10'' high, **$90-$100.**

POPEYE COLLECTIBLES

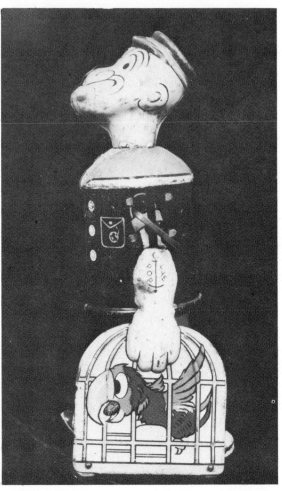

POPEYE AND THE PARROT CAGES, tin mechanical windup, Marx, 1930s, **$65-$75.**

POPEYE-IN-A-ROWBOAT, hand-cranked, 1935, 15'' long, rare, **$1300-$1500.** POPEYE PATROL MOTORCYCLE, cast iron, Hubley, 1938, 9'' long, **$80-$90.** POPEYE EXPRESS, pushing wheelbarrow, lithographed tin, Marx, 1930s, **$175-$200.** POPEYE EXPRESS, he's in airplane, lithographed tin, Marx, 1930s, rare, **$450-$500.** POPEYE IN A BARREL, Chien, 1930s, 7'' high, **$180-$200.** WALKING POPEYE, Chien, 1930s, **$240-$270.**

PUPPETS

LITHOGRAPHED PAPER ON WOOD, you assembled them, joints moved, late 1800s, **$70-$90** set of two.

CHARLIE McCARTHY HAND-TYPE, cloth, 1930s, **$15-$20.** WOODEN FIGURE, strings operated it, 1920s, **$25-$30.** "HOWDY DOODY" HAND-TYPE, cloth, 1950s, **$4-$6.**

PROJECTORS

TIN, Hand-operated, concave mirror at rear, 1920s, 6" high, **$45-$55.**

PUZZLES

"TRAIN," cardboard, Milton-Bradley, Springfield, Massachusetts, early 1900s, **$18-$25.**

"PASTIME" PUZZLE, Parker Brothers, 1932-1957, **$14-$16.**

"WIZARD OF OZ" CHARACTERS, cardboard on wood, 1940s, **$12-$16.** "MICKEY MOUSE," cardboard, 1930s, **$17-$22.** "WHITE HOUSE," cardboard, 1920s, **$20-$28.** "TOM MIX," cardboard, radio premium, 1920s, **$22-$30.**

—Q—

—R—

RABBITS

FRENCH MECHANICAL WINDUP, early 1900s, **$75-$85**.

TIN MECHANICAL WINDUP, 1940s, **$20-$25**.

WOODEN PULL TOY, 1930s, 9'' long, **$12-$15**. RABBIT PULLING EASTER BASKET, mechanical windup, 1940s, **$20-$25**.

RACERS

CAST IRON RACER, early 1900s, **$45-$55**; with driver, **$85-$95**.

TIN FRICTION, occupied Japan, 1940s, **$12-$18**.

MOODY'S NEW RACER, by Moody and Company, Chicago, Illinois, 1870, in several sizes, **$250-$275**.

INDY 500, tin mechanical windup, 1930s, **$35-$45**. WOODEN PUSH (carpet) TOY, painted, 1930s, **$25-$35**. AUTOMOBILE AND DRIVER, cast iron, Hubley, 1900s, **$40-$50**. CAST IRON AUTOMOBILE, No. 684, Hubley, 1900s, 8½'' long, **$45-$55**. CAST IRON, cast wheels, 1900s, 6¼'' long, **$45-$55**.

RATTLES

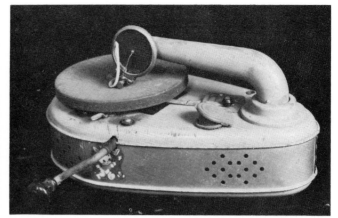

RECORD PLAYERS

TIN, windup, plays, 1940s, 9" long, **$35-$45.**

REINS

TOY "HORSE" REINS, made of rope, bells on headband, worn by boys playing "horsey," 1882, **$20-$30** pair.

WOODEN, painted, Germany, 1900s, **$8-$10** each.

REFRIGERATORS

BRASS BABY RATTLE, bells-on-wooden handle, 1800s, **$28-$35.**

LITHOGRAPH ON CARDBOARD, wooden handle, 1900s, **$5-$7.**

PLASTIC "STRING OF BEADS," eight in string, 1940s, **$3-$6.**

SALESMAN'S SAMPLES (illus.), cast iron, 1920s, 4" and 6" high, **$12-$18** each. LITTLE ORPHAN ANNIE, tin, 1930s, 4" high, **$60-$70.**

—S—

SANTA CLAUS

BAG FILLED WITH MINIATURE TOYS, he walks, tin clockwork mechanism, 1882, 9½" high, **$125-$150.**

SCALES

CAST IRON TOY SCALES, painted, tin scoop and iron weights, 1882, 8" long, **$35-$45.**

REINDEER

POT METAL, bells-on-strap around neck, late 1800s, 6" high, **$11-$20.**

RIDING TOY

WOODEN RIDING TOY, 1850s, **$350-$500.**

MARY'S LITTLE LAMB, saddle cloth and bridle, 1880s, **$300-$350.** THE MECHANICAL HAND VELOCIPEDE AND RIDER, 1882, **$325-$375.**

RUBBER TOYS

PAINTED DOG, PAINTED CAT, PAINTED SHEEP, with whistles, just squeeze, 1892, 3½" long, **$8-$10** each; in plain finish, **$6-$8** each.

SCHOENHUT

CAMEL, 1924, **$45-$55.** ELEPHANT (see cover), **$45-$55.** GIRAFFE, 1924, **$55-$65.**

PULL TOYS, bells in wheels, 1920s, **$100-$125.**

CLOWN FIGURES, 1934, **$35-$45.**

This simply marvelous company deserves a few lines all its own. Albert Schoenhut began building toys and pianos in 1872. His dolls first appeared in 1911, a walking doll in 1913. His greatest triumph was his Humpty Dumpty Circus, The Toy Wonder—10,001 new tricks with unbreakable jointed figures. Today an oblong tent with about 40 pieces—clowns, animals, acrobatic equipment—brings $4,000 to $5,000. And rightfully so! He was great—his family still is. Mr. Schoenhut passed away in 1924. What a man!

See them all at the Museum of Yesterday's Toys, St. George Street, in St. Augustine, Florida!

SCOOP

CHILD'S CRANBERRY SCOOP, hand-carved, mid-1800s. Not all child-size objects were playthings. The kids pitched in too! **$95-$120.**

SECTIONAL BLOCKS

SET OF SECTIONAL BLOCKS, cardboard, all letters of alphabet can be made as well as other structures, by Crandall, 1882, **$95-$110.**

SEESAWS

See Teeter-Totters.

SEWING MACHINES

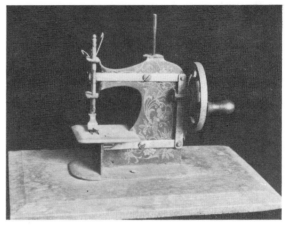

CHILD'S SIZE, early 1900s, **$18-$22.**

SINGER, child-size, original box, etc., **$30-$40.**
WHITE, child-size, original box, **$25-$30.**
FAIRY "HOOP" TYPE, cast iron, makes elastic loop stitches, 1882, **$50-$60.**

SHIPS

COMPOSITION WITH CLOTH SAILS (illus.), 1920s, **$18-$28.** WOODEN TAKE-APART, pull type, 1930s, **$12-$15.**

SHOOTING GAME OF RINALDO

THREE GAMES: "The Chase," "National Standard," "Junior Creedmore," boxed, with full instructions, 1882, **$95-$100** all.

SKATES

WOOD/IRON, hand-forged, no straps, 1880s, **$22-$27** pair.

WOODEN WHEELS, leather backs and straps, 1910, **$35-$45** pair.

CHILD'S, hard rubber wheels, 1950s, **$8-$12** pair.

SLATES

"LITTLE MISS," company giveaway sample, 1900s. Western Washboard Sales, Chicago, prospered until the electric washer appeared. Oh, progress! **$10-$12.**

HANDMADE SLATE, 1900s, **$4-$6.**

BLACKBOARD, with crank-type paper pics, 1920s, **$25-$30.**

SLEDS

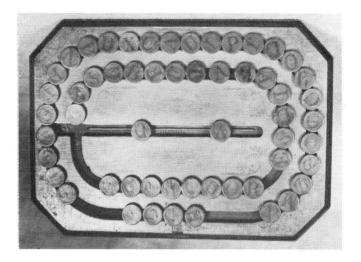

CHILD'S WOOD/METAL SLED, hand-painted, 1920s, 33" long, **$75-$85.**

FLEXIBLE FLYER, 1930s, different sizes, **$18-$20.** WOODEN, turned up runners, 1900s, **$30-$40.**

SOUVENIR ITEMS

MINIATURE CREAMER AND WATER SPRINK-LER, Germany, 1900s, **$6-8** each.

"NIAGRA FALLS" PLATE, 1920s, 2½" in diameter, **$3-$4.** "CHICAGO" SUGAR BOWL, 1930s, 3" high, **$2-$3.** "I LOVE MISSY" TUMBLER, 1920s, **$3-$4.**

SPELLING BOARDS

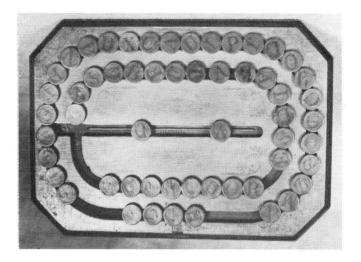

WOODEN, patented February 1886, **$45-$55.**

SPINNING TOY

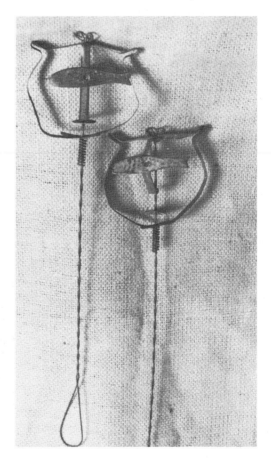

PRIMITIVE "SPINNING" TOY, late 1800s, **$7-$9** each.

81

STAGECOACH

POT METAL, two riders, 1920s, **$85-$95.**

TIN MECHANICAL WINDUP, lithographed, 1930s, 4½'' high, **$45-$55.** WOODEN PULL TOY, painted, rider is removable, 1920s, 14'' long, **$60-$70.** "WELLS FARGO," Tootsietoy, 1920s, **$35-$45.**

STEAM ENGINES

HORIZONTAL, heated electrically, throttle, etc., on boiler, Weeden, early 1900s, **$125-$150.**

HORIZONTAL, Weeden Company, New Bedford, Massachusetts, early 1900s, **$150-$200.** LOCOMOTIVE, possibly by E. Beggs, 1900s, **$250-$300.** UPRIGHT, tin boiler, late 1800s, 7'' high, **$200-$225.** HORIZONTAL, heated with electricity, by Weeden, 1900s, 7¼'' long, **$125-$150.** UPRIGHT, with vertical boiler and a whistle, early 1900s, 10'' high, **225-$250.**

UPRIGHT, small alcohol burner fires boiler, made by Weeden, 1900s, **$100-$125.**

STEAM ROLLERS

TIN BUDDY L "RIDER" TYPE, 1930s, 12½'' high, **$50-$75.**

LIVE STEAM-TYPE, electrically operated, early 1900s, 9'' high, **$125-$150.** CAST IRON, Hubley, early 1900s, 5'' long, **$12-$18.** CAST IRON, painted early 1900s, 6½'' long, **$18-$20.**

STEREOPTICONS (Stereoscopes)

BUCKEYE STEREOPTICON COMPANY, Cleveland, Ohio, 1900s, **$35-$45.**

STEREOSCOPE, with 12 cards, English, 1860s, **$55-$85.** STEREOSCOPE, with 300 cards, 1900s, **$125-$155.** STEREOSCOPE, with 75 cards in box, Civil War scenes, rare, **$200-$250.** STEREOSCOPE, "Saturnscope," table model, walnut stand, 1892, **$80-$100.** EXTRA CARDS, various scenes, 1860s to 1915, **$1-$3** each. Note: If cards are warped, moisten backside, then press gently on backside with warm (not hot) iron on flat surface. Then place heavy book on backside for an hour or so. You're welcome!

STEINS

MINIATURE POT METAL, graniteware, late 1800s, 2¼" high, **$4-$5.**

PEWTER, English, late 1800s, 4½" high, **$75-$100.** MINIATURE POT METAL, painted, early 1900s, 2-1/8" high, **$6-$8.** PEWTER, lithograph in bottom, German, early 1900s, 4" high, **$85-$95.**

STONES

AMERICAN/GERMAN ARCHITECTURAL ANCHOR BOX, complete with instruction book, in wooden box, stones in three colors, late 1800s, **$65-$85.**

STOVES (Ranges)

"CRESCENT" CAST IRON, early 1900s, 5" high, **$65-$75.**

NO. 893S NICKEL-PLATED, Hubley, 1900s, 3¾" long, 4¾" high, **$55-$65.**

RODER SALESMAN'S SAMPLE, cast iron, 1920s, **$18-$28.** LITTLE ORPHAN ANNIE STOVE, tin, radio premium, **$35-$45.**

WILKENS CAST IRON RANGE, No. 201, 1895, 16" high, **$75-$85.** WILKENS CAST IRON STOVE, No. 200, 1895, 9½" wide, **$65-$75.** ELECTRO-OXIDIZED "EAGLE" RANGE, No. 879C, Hubley, 1900s, 19" high, **$75-$85.** NICKEL-PLATED "BABY" RANGE, Hubley, 1900s, 4-1/8" high, **$45-$55.** NICKEL-PLATED "EAGLE" RANGE, No. 840, Hubley, 1900s, 7" high, **$60-$70.** IMPLEMENTS FOR STOVES, **$3-$6** each.

STREETCARS (Trolleys)

TIN PULL TOY, Lehmann, 1890s, 8" long, **$95-$125.**

CAST IRON, clockwork windup, 1910, 9" long, **$65-$75.** TIN, friction monorail, Lehmann, 1912, **$75-$80.** TIN PULL TOY, possibly Converse, Winchendon, Massachusetts, late 1800s, **$125-$155.** TIN, lithographed, Chien, London, 1910s, 8½" long, **$120-$135.**

"SPARK" POT BELLY, cast iron, no stack, 1900s, 12½" high, **$50-$60.**

TIN, friction, doors open and close, late 1800s, **$85-$95.**

TIN PULL TOY, open-air, 1890s, **$125-$150.**

SULKYS

CAST IRON, Hubley-type pull toy, early 1900s, 8½'' long, **$150-$165.**

CAST IRON, 1920s, **$65-$85.**

CAST IRON SULKY PLOW, No. 410, Wilkens, 1895, 10½" long, **$125-$150.** CAST IRON SULKY, No. 165, Wilkens, 1895, 9" long, **$145-$160.** CAST IRON SULKY, No. 208, Hubley "Lancaster," 1906, 6" long, **$135-$145.** CAST IRON SULKY, No. 72, Hubley "Lancaster," 1906, 8¼" long, **$125-$145.** CAST IRON SULKY, No. 31, Hubley "Lancaster," 7½" long, **$125-$145.**

SUPERMAN

SUPERMAN FIGHTING AIRPLANE, Tin mechanical windup, lithographed, Marx, 1940, 6" long, **$150-$200.** SUPERMAN COMIC BOOK, 1939, **$60-$70.** SUPERMAN COMIC BOOKS, 1940s and 1950s, **$8-$10** each. SUPERMAN T-SHIRT, 1950s, **$4-$6.**

SWANS

HOLLOW TIN PULL TOY, on wheels, late 19th century, **$170-$200.**

SWEEPERS

"LITTLE DAISY," made by Bissell for give-aways, 1920s, 28½" long. It works! **$15-$20.**

—T—

TAXIS

CAST IRON, Arcadia, painted, 1928, 5" long, **$100-$125.**

CAST IRON, Raher, stubby construction, 1920s, 7½" long, **$100-$125.** AMOS 'N ANDY FRESH AIR CAB, see Amos 'n Andy. TIN MECHANICAL WINDUP, lithographed, Marx, 1930s, **$80-$90.** CAST IRON, No. 353, Hubley, 1900s, 5½" long, **$85-$95.**

TEA SETS

PORCELAIN, six-piece, Japan, 1920s, tallest 2" high, **$30-$35** set.

PORCELAIN, hand-painted, Japan (Nippon), 1900s, **$40-$50** set.

TIN, lithographed, 1920s, **$23-$33** set.

ALICE-IN-WONDERLAND, plastic, 12-piece, 1930s, **$20-$30** set. IRONSTONE, seven-piece, Johnson, England, 1920s, **$28-$35**.

TIN, painted, eight-piece, Germany, 1910, **$35-$45** set. SANDWICH GLASS, seven-piece, lacy pattern, 1850s, rare, **$275-$325** set.

TEETER-TOTTERS (Seesaws)

"BUSY BEE," tin mechanical, lithographed, sand operates, 1920s, **$65-$75**.

"CLOWNS-ON-ROCKER," tin, mechanical, 1900s, **$95-$120**. "MAMA KATZENJAMMER AND PROFESSOR SEESAW," pull toy, by Kenton Hardware Manufacturing Company, Kenton, Ohio, 1900s, **$125-$155**. "MONKIES ON A TEETER," tin, clockwork, Germany, 1900s, **$70-$90**.

TIN, mechanical, painted, patented September 15, 1903, **$85-$95**.

TIC-TAC-TOE

WOODEN PRIMITIVE, New Hampshire, 1890s. Still being made. This is a reproduction, 1930s. **$12-$18**.

TIGER

PAPIER-MACHE, nodding head and tail, Chinese, 1930s, **$25-$35**.

TOILET AND JEWELRY SET

FRENCH, 13 pieces, 1882, **$125-$150** complete.

TEMPLE TOY

BRASS, India, mid-19th century, **$85-$95**.

TOPS

WOODEN, 1900s, 2''-2½'' high, **$10-$15** each.

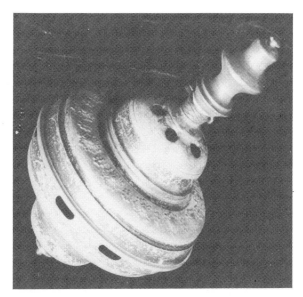

TIN PUSH/PULL-TYPE, painted, musical, 1930s, **$18-$28.**

WOODEN, 1920s to 1930s, different sizes, **$6-$11** each. CASTING OR PEG-TYPE, 1890s, **$9-$12** each. IVORY HUMMING-TYPE, 1850s, **$50-$60.**

TORPEDO GUN

GATHMANN, rubber bands propel the torpedo, 11" long, **$80-$90.** U.S. NAVY PATTERN, 1892, 15" long, **$120-$135.**

TOTEM POLES

CHILD'S, hand-carved wood, from Alaska, 1880s, 28" high, **$35-$45.**

CHILD'S, composition, Japan, 1930s, 26" high, **$8-$10.** CHILD'S, wooden, Germany, 1930s, 18" high, **$5-$9.**

TOY PEDDLER

TIN MECHANICAL WINDUP, Germany, 1930s, 6½" high. Mickey Mouse is missing at bottom of string. That's right, Herr Von Mouse himself!, **$85-$95;** with Mickey Mouse, **$150-$175.**

TRACTORS

CAST IRON, driver missing, 1920s, 6" long, **$25-$35.**

89

POT METAL, 1930s, 2½" long, **$25-$35.**

CAST IRON, Arcade, caterpillar, chain tread, 1920s, 5½" long, **$35-$45.** CAST IRON SHOVEL-TYPE, driver missing, 1920s, 9½" long, **$85-$95.** CAST IRON "AVERY," No. 320, Hubley "Lancaster," 1910s, 5" long, **$70-$90.** TIN, climbing type, mechanical windup, lithographed, Marx, 1920s, **$45-$55.** CAST METAL, diesel type, wooden wheels, Tootsie-toy, 1930s, **$25-$35.**

"TRAFFIC B"

SQUAD CAR, tin mechanical windup, Marx, 1930s, **$65-$75.**

TRAINS

TIN, lithographed, mid-1800s, 7" long, **$200-$250.**

CAST IRON ENGINE AND COAL TENDER, "Iron Art," J. M. 240 R, 1900s, **$65-$75** both.

ENGINE AND COAL TENDER, tin/wood, 1930s, **$35-$45.**

MINIATURE TIN, lithographed, late 1800s, 6½'' long, **$125-$150.**

POT METAL, four-piece, 1920s, 8'' long, **$65-$75** all.

LITHOGRAPH ON WOOD, three-piece, 1850s, **$125-$150** all.

''O'' GAUGE, pot metal type, electric, four-piece set, 1950s on, with 10 feet of track, **$75-$95** set.

CAST IRON ENGINE AND CAR, early 1900s, **$60-$80** both.

"GNB—BAVARIA," tin, electric headlight works, circular track, early 1900s, **$100-$150** all.

CAST IRON LOCOMOTIVE, No. 919, mechanical windup, Wilkens, 1885, 9½" long, **$95-$120**. CAST IRON PASSENGER TRAIN, No. 995, Wilkens, 1885, 29" long **$175-$225**. POLISHED COPPER OXIDIZED PASSENGER TRAIN, No. 60½, Hubley, 1900s, 43" long, **$180-$220**.

TREES

PALM TREE, cast lead, German, 1900s, 3" high, **$2-$3** each. MAPLE, alloy, English, 1920s, 2½" high, **$1-$2** each. OAK, cast lead, German, 1920s, 2½" high, **$1-$2** each.

TRICYCLES

"TOM THUMB," metal, wooden hubs and spokes, 1910, **$175-$225**.

METAL, 1900s, 26" high, **$125-$150**. COMPOSITION DOLL, 1940s, 28" high, **$60-$70**.

ELECTRIC, steel, made by Ayrtar and Perry, 1880s, **$1,000 and up.**

IRISH MAIL VELOCIPEDE, 1910, **$300-$350.**

ALL-STEEL, steel or rubber tires, 1902, **$75-$90.** ENAMELED BLACK METAL, rubber tires, upholstered seat, 1902, **$95-$125.**

TROLLS

HARD RUBBER, synthetic hair, Swedish, 1950s, 4" high, **$4-$6.** Just what these are all about and why they became so popular throughout the world is a mystery to me!

TOONERVILLE TROLLEY

TIN MECHANICAL WINDUP, copyright 1922 by Fontaine Fox, made by Nifty in 1922, 6¾" high, 5" long, **$250-$275.**

TRACK-TYPE windup, made to run on tracks, five different sizes were made, **$225-$250.**

TRUCKS

WOODEN PULL TOY, early 1900s, **$100-$125.**

METAL BUDDY "L" TRUCK, 1920s, **$85-$95.**

METAL KEYSTONE PACKARD WATER TRUCK, has steering mechanism and rubber tires, 1920s, 33" long, **$65-$75.**

DELIVERY TRUCK, cast iron, 1930s, **$45-$55.**

TIN, Metalcraft Corp., St. Louis, 1930s, **$65-$75.**

TIN FIRE TRUCK, ladder, Germany, 1940s, **$65-$85.**

PLASTIC U.S. ARMY TRUCK, 1940s, **$25-$35.**

TIN STRUCTO FARMS, Structo Manufacturing, Freeport, Illinois, 1940s, **$30-$40.**

CAST IRON "AUTO EXPRESS" TRUCK, No. 737 L, Hubley, 1900s, **$90-$100.** CAST IRON COAL TRUCK, No. 784, Hubley, 1900s, **$90-$100.** METAL BUDDY "L" DUMP TRUCK, dump works, 1920s, 23" long, **$70-$85.**

TIN HOWARD JOHNSON'S, 1950s, **$25-$35.**

TRUNKS

TUBS

WOOD, cloth-covered, leather strips, late 1800s, **$18-$25.**

WOOD, paper-covered, lock, late 1800s, 5½" wide, **$15-$22.**

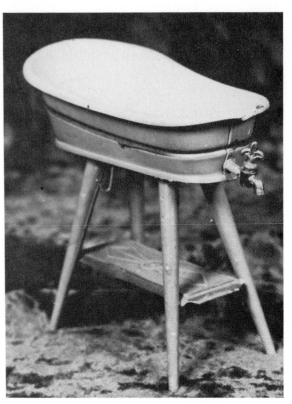

TIN TUB-ON-WOODEN STAND, drain spout works, early 1900s, 6½" high, **$10-$12.** TIN, floor-type, painted, late 1800s, 5" long, **$18-$25.**

—U—

UNCLE TOM'S CABIN

CABIN, family, pets, fence and buildings are blocks, 1880s, 11" long, **$125-$140.**

UNCLE WIGGILY'S CRAZY CAR, 1920s, Germany, **$950-$1000.** UNCLE WIGGILY CAR by Marx, 1935, **$125-$150.**

—V—

CAMELBACK, wood, paper-covered, late 1800s, 6" wide, **$15-$22.**

—W—

WAGONS

WOODEN, primitive (handmade), pull toy, 1920s, **$35-$45**.

TIN/WOOD PULL TOY, early 1900s, **$75-$85**.

TIN PULL TOY, large, **$18-$22**; small, **$8-$12**.

CAST IRON BAND WAGON, No. 789, Hubley, 1900s, 30'' long, **$375-$400**. CAST IRON COAL WAGON, No. 121, Hubley, 1900s, 16½'' long, **$150-$175**. CAST IRON EXPRESS WAGON, No. 175, Wilkens, 1895, 14'' long, **$195-$225**. CAST IRON GROCERY WAGON, No. 176, Wilkens, 1895, 14'' long, **$195-$225**. CAST IRON ROYAL CIRCUS TIGER CAGE WAGON, Hubley, 1920, **$295-$350**. CAST IRON BAND WAGON, Hubley, 1920s, **$450-$500**.

TIN, canvas top, lithographed wooden horses, pull toy, 1870s, **$125-$150**.

CAST IRON "CHAMPION EXPRESS," rubber wheels, 1930s, 10'' long, **$25-$35**.

CAST IRON FARM, early 1900s, 6½'' long, **$35-$45**.

WAREHOUSE

THREE STORIES HIGH, complete with windlass, scales, platform truck, 1880s, 17" high, **$125-$150.**

WASHDAY

MINIATURE, wooden, handmade, 1940s, 2" and 3", **$4-$5** each.

WEATHERVANES

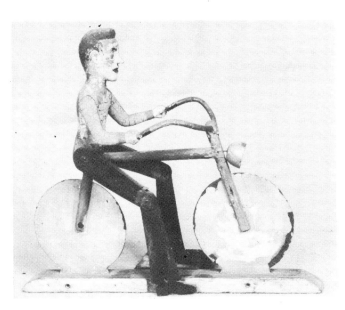

PRIMITIVE, made by or for a boy, early 1900s, **$65-$85.**

WHEELBARROWS

WOODEN, 1920s, 18" long, **$10-$15.**

TIN, 1920s, 29" long, **$35-$45.** GARDEN TOOLS, **$15-$18** set.

WHIRLIGIGS

SOLDIER, 19th century, 28" high, **$750-$800.**

TOP-HATTED MAN, mid-19th century, 16" high, **$750-$800.**

WHISTLES

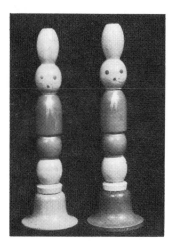

"RABBIT," wooden, 1930s, 8½" long, **$7-$9** each.

TIN, in shape of canary, 1900s, **$20-$25.**
METAL, police-type, cork inside, 1930s, **$8-$12.**

WINDMILL

STEAM-OPERATED, with stationary engine, 1892, 11" high, **$195-$200.**

—X—

—Y—

—Z—

ZOETROPE

GERMAN, 1880s. It's said Edison got the idea for his first motion picture machine from watching one of these. **$95-$100** with paper inserts.

TOY MANUFACTURERS IN AMERICA BEFORE 1900

Though I have attempted to be as accurate as possible, the publisher and I disclaim any responsibility for specific company names and dates.

American Doll and Toy Company
New York, New York
1860s; toy jobbers

American Toy Company
Newark, New Jersey
1890s; toys

American Toy Watch Company
Providence, Rhode Island
1860s; toy watches

Arnold Print Works
North Adams, Massachusetts
Late 1800s; printed cloth for stuffing toy figures—animals, etc.

Artz and Sons
New York, New York
1880s; toys

Atlas Gun Company
Ilion, New York
1890s; air rifles

Automatic Toy Works
New York, New York
Late 1800s; windup toys

Bacon and Priestly
Grand Rapids, Michigan
Late 1800s; sleds

Baker and Wilson
Templeton, Massachusetts
After Civil War to late 1800s; wagons, toy carriages

Barker, Jones and Fargo
Sandisfield, Massachusetts
Late 1860s; sleds, toy carts, hoops

Barnes and Company
Covington, Kentucky
Late 1870s; bicycles

Barney and Barry
Springfield, Massachusetts
1860s; skates (roller and ice)

Baseball Emporium Manufacturing Company
New York, New York
Mid-1860s; indoor and outdoor croquet, bats

Beiser and Company
New York, New York
1890s; toy soldiers

Bethel Toy Manufacturing Company
Bethel, Vermont
Early 1880s; toys

Bevin Brothers
East Hampton, Connecticut
1830s; bells, bell toys; the East Hampton Bell Company made most of the bells used on U.S. Navy craft up to the Korean War

Bliss and Company
Providence, Rhode Island
Mid-1840s; tool chests, blocks, doll houses, etc.

Booth and Rockwell
Monroeton, Pennsylvania
Late 1800s; come-back balls, tops, bats, etc.

Bradley, Milton, Company
Springfield, Massachusetts
1860s on; trains, games, puzzles, guns, etc.

Brandenstein, B.
New York, New York
1860s; dolls

Brown, George W., and Company
Forestville and Bristol, Connecticut
Late 1860s; tin and windup toys; owned American Toy Company, New York, New York, for a short time

Brown and Eggleston
New York, New York
1850s; carriage, hobby horses, etc.

Buckman Manufacturing Company
New York, New York
Late 1860s; toys, toy guns, steam engines

Buffalo Toy Works
Buffalo, New York
Late 1800s; metal toys

Bush and Spencer
Springfield, Massachusetts
Mid-1860s; toy drums

Carlisle and Finch
Cincinnati, Ohio
Late 1800s; electric trains

Carrom Industries
Ludington, Michigan
Early 1880s; toys, wooden games

Chase Stockinet Doll Company
Pawtucket, Rhode Island
1890s; dolls

Christian, A.
New York, New York
1850s on; sleds, bicycles, hobby horses, etc.;
several firms involved here, until 1880s

Clark, Austin and Smith
New York, New York
1860s; paper dolls

Clay, R. J.
New York, New York
Late 1860s; windup toys, etc.; founded
Automatic Toy Works, later purchased by
Ives of Bridgeport, Connecticut

Clayton Brothers
Bristol, Connecticut
Late 1800s; skates

Coe and Sniffen
Stratford, Connecticut
Late 1850s until after Civil War; skates

Cole and Ballard
Newark, New Jersey
1870s; carriages, sleds, etc.

Coleman and Company
New York, New York
Late 1800s; toys

Converse, M.
Winchendon, Massachusetts
1870s; drums, wooden blocks, toys, hobby
horses, etc.

Cox and Stephens
New York, New York
1880s; toys

Crandall (father, brothers, sons)
New York, New York
Early 1840s until after 1900; every type toy

Crosby, Nichols and Company
Boston, Massachusetts
1850s; children's books, paper dolls

Crown Roller Skate Company
Chicago, Illinois
1880s on; roller skates

Daisy Manufacturing Company
Rogers, Arkansas
Late 1880s; toy guns, air rifles; originally in
Plymouth, Michigan

Dickinson and Thayer
Hadley, Massachusetts
Late 1840s until after Civil War; wagons
carriages

Dotter Doll Company
Brooklyn, New York
Late 1800s; dolls

Dubuar Manufacturing Company
Northville, Michigan
1890s; air rifles; a firm taken over by Daisy
in early 1900s

Eagle Manufacturing Company
Grand Rapids, Michigan
Late 1880s; sleds

Eagle Augur and Skate Company
Wallingford, Connecticut
1870s; skates

East Hampton Bell Company
See Bevin Brothers

Edison Phonograph Toy Manufacturing
Company
New York, New York
1890; talking dolls (one of the rarest dolls in
the world today)

Elder and Brown
New York, New York
Mid-1860s, 1870s; wagons, hobby horses, etc.

Ellis, Joel
Vermont
Credited with carving some of the first
wooden dolls in America

Ellis, Britton and Eaton
Springfield, Vermont
1860s to 1890s; wooden dolls, wooden toys,
etc.; apparently related to Joel Ellis

Euler and Company
Louisville, Kentucky
1860s; toys; some say the firm made candy

Eureka Manufacturing Company
Boston, Massachusetts
1870s; air pistols

Ewing and Quinn
New York, New York
After Civil War until 1880s; doll trunks

Fairweather, Tillie
Hartford, Connecticut
Late 1800s; doll dresses

Featherstone, A., and Company
Chicago, Illinois
1890s; toys

Feust and Rice
New York, New York
1870s; toys

Fletcher and Webster
Nashua, New Hampshire
1865 until late 1880s; wood and tin toys

Fraley, G. W., and Company
Philadelphia, Pennsylvania
1870s; bicycles

Fuller and Davis
Worthington, Massachusetts
1850s; wagons, carriages

Garton Toy Company
Sheboygan, Wisconsin
1870s; toys; several variations of firm name;
issued first toy catalog under name of Garton
Toy Company, 1887

Gibbs Manufacturing Company
Canton, Ohio
Late 1800s; tops, push and pull toys

Glascock Brothers
Muncie, Indiana
1890s; toy washing machines, etc.

Gong Bell Manufacturing Company
See Bevins Brothers

Gormully and Jeffery
Chicago, Illinois
Late 1800s; bicycles

Greiner, Ludwig
Philadelphia, Pennsylvania
1840s until 1870s; dolls, doll heads; he took
out the first U.S. patent on a doll's head in
1858

Hahne and Block
Newark, New Jersey
1850s; toys

Halley Manufacturing Company
Salisbury, Connecticut
1870s; pocket knives

Hayden and Chester
Providence, Rhode Island
Late 1800s; toys

Hersey
South Hingham, Massachusetts
1840s to 1880s; several members of the same
family who made wooden toys

Heywood Brothers
Gardner, Massachusetts
1820s until 1890s; toy furniture, carriages

Hoffman-Knickerbocker Company
Albany, New York
1850s; alphabet and lithographed wooden
blocks

Home Music Company
Providence, Rhode Island
1880s; mechanical and musical toys

Houghton and Edson
Hudson, Massachusetts
1860s; wooden toys, blocks, toy safes

Hovey, J. G.
Boston, Massachusetts
1840s; one of the early manufacturers
of fireworks

Hubley Manufacturing Company
Lancaster, Pennsylvania
1890s; iron toys, guns

Hurley and Simond
Haverhill, Massachusetts
Early 1880s; toys

Hyatt and Company
Newark, New Jersey
1860s to 1880s; celluloid dolls, heads and
bodies, some with real hair wigs

Ideal Manufacturing Company
Detroit, Michigan
1890s; iron toys, trains

Ives, E. R., and Company
Plymouth and Bridgeport, Connecticut
1860s; trains, mechanical windup toys, etc.;
several firm names; took over various firms,
such as Automatic Toy Works, New York,
New York, once known as Ives, Blakeslee
and Williams

Jacobs and Pettibone
Cincinnati, Ohio
1870s; toys

Jarves, Deming
Sandwich, Massachusetts
1825; doll dishes

Johnston and Company
New York, New York
Late 1880s; doll carriages, toys; also agents
for other toy manufacturers

Kaldenberg and Company
New York, New York
1890s; rubber toys

Kenton Hardware Company
Kenton, Ohio
1880s; iron toys, toy banks

Kimmel and Forster
New York, New York
1860s; paper dolls

Kingsbury Manufacturing Company
Keene, New Hampshire
1890s; banks, iron toys, windup toys

Kipp Brothers
Louisville, Kentucky
1890s; toys

Kirby and Fountain
Middletown, Connecticut
Late 1880s; bell toys, toy trunks, etc.

Klingman, Sturdevan Larrabee
Binghamton, New York
Late 1880s; sleds, carriages

Knapp Electric Company
New York, New York
1890s; electric trains, toys

Knost Brothers
Cincinnati, Ohio
1870s; celluloid toys; Licht and Wankelman
took this firm over about 1895

Lancaster, G. H.
Philadelphia, Pennsylvania
1890s; toy whips

Lauterbach, H. G.
Boston, Massachusetts
Mid-1870s; tin toys; also imported and
retailed toys

Lawrence, H.
Brooklyn, New York
1880s; drums, toys, musical toys

Lerch and Klagg
Philadelphia, Pennsylvania
1860s; doll heads

Lesser and Company
New York, New York
1860s; toys

Lloyd Manufacturing Company
Minneapolis, Minnesota
Late 1800s; wagons, doll carts, etc.

Lockwood Manufacturing Company
South Norwalk, Connecticut
1880s; iron toys

Lovell Arms Company
Boston, Massachusetts
1870s to 1890s; skates, bicycles, etc.

Ludlow Toy Manufacturing Company
Ludlow, Vermont
1870s to 1890s; wagons, doll buggies, etc.

Lyman and Curtiss
New York, New York
1880s; toys

Lynch and Son
Providence, Rhode Island
1860s; sleds, doll furniture

McKee and Harrington
Hackensack, New Jersey
1880s; toys

Manhattan Doll Company
New York, New York
1890s; dolls

Markham Manufacturing Company
Plymouth, Michigan
1880s; a company taken over by
Daisy in 1913

Martin and Rippel
New York, New York
1880s; toys, dolls; Wiegand joined
firm in 1883

Mason Manufacturing Company
Gardner, Massachusetts
1890s; doll furniture, wooden toys; moved
to Paris, Maine, about 1903

Mead, A. F.
New York, New York
1880s; toys

Meinecke, A., and Company
Milwaukee, Wisconsin
1850s; doll carriages, toy furniture, etc.

Mercer and Monod
New York, New York
Late 1860s; bicycles

Merriam Manufacturing Company
Durham, Connecticut
After Civil War to 1880s; tin toys

Metzler and Cowperthwaite
New York, New York
Mid-1860s; hobby horses

Mishler, M. B.
Ravenna, Ohio
1890s; marbles

Monarch Bicycles
New York, New York; Chicago, Illinois;
San Francisco, California
1890s; bicycles

Moore Manufacturing Company
Kensington, Connecticut
1870s; wooden toys, etc.

Moulton, J. L.
Lowell, Massachusetts
1880s; croquet

Mueller and Sinsheimer
New York, New York
1870s; toys

Murdock and Company
Winchendon, Massachusetts
Late 1870s; wooden toys

National Toy Company
New York, New York
1870s; toys

Navarre Glass Marble Company
Navarre, Ohio
1890s; marbles

New Brunswick Rubber Company
New York, New York
1850s; India rubber toys

New England Toy Company
Providence, Rhode Island
Late 1860s; toy watches, toy clocks,
tin toy furniture, etc.

New York Rubber Company
New York, New York
1890s; toys, rubber dolls

Noble and Cooley
Granville, Massachusetts
1850s; toys, drums

Novelty Manufacturing Company
Chicago, Illinois
1870s; carts, carriages, sleds, wagons, etc.;
firm also known as Steam Works of Chicago

Oppenheim, F. M.
New York, New York
1890s; toys

Overman, A. H., Wheel Company
New York, New York; Boston, Massachusetts;
Detroit, Michigan; and other cities
Late 1800s; bicycles; made the first
American safety bicycle

Parker Brothers
Salem, Massachusetts
1883 on; games. Who hasn't heard of
this great company?

Partridge, H.
Providence, Rhode Island
Mid-1860s; toy flags, toy books, fireworks,
toys, etc.

Partridge, H., and Company
Chicago, Illinois
1890s; toys

Peabody and Whitney
Boston, Massachusetts
1878; wheel toys; jobbers, retailers;
took over Bridgman and Peabody

Peck and Baker
Springfield, Massachusetts
1870s; toy gigs, etc.

Philadelphia Tin Toy Manufacturing Company
Philadelphia, Pennsylvania
Late 1840s to 1850s; tin toys; firm also known
as Francis, Field and Francis

Philadelphia Toboggan Company
Germantown, Pennsylvania
Mid-1800s; carousel animals, etc.

Pia, Peter
New York, New York
Late 1840s; trains, toy furniture, etc.; at least
four names involved here from
beginning to 1880s

Pierce, J. A.
Chicago, Illinois
1870s; steam engines, steamboats,
mechanical toys, etc.

Pope Manufacturing Company
Boston, Massachusetts
Late 1870s; one of the world's
great bicycle manufacturers

Pratt and Letchworth
Buffalo, New York
1890s; toys

Quackenbush, H. W.
Herkimer, New York
1870s; toy guns, pistols, building blocks.
Yes, Groucho, there **was** a Quackenbush!

Rice and Randall
Marlboro, Massachusetts
1860s; toys

Richardson Ball Bearing Skate Company
Chicago, Illinois
Late 1880s; roller skates

Robinson, L.
Bristol, Connecticut
1849 to 1850; wagons; Case and Robinson
after 1851

Rogers, C., and Company
Norwich, Connecticut
1870s; skates

Rubber Tipped Arrow Company
Boston, Massachusetts
1890s; dart pistols

St. Louis Refrigerator and
Wood Cutter Company
St. Louis, Missouri
1890s; toys; most folks knew it
as the St. Louis Toy Company

St. Nicholas Manufacturing Company
Chicago, Illinois
1890s; toys

Schmidt Toy and Wheel Company
Chicago, Illinois
1890s; toys

Schoenhut, A., Company
Philadelphia, Pennsylvania
1872; dolls, musical instruments, multi-jointed
animals ("Humpty Dumpty" Circus, after
1903); firm still in business; one of the greats

Sears, A. T.
Chicago, Illinois
1880s; velocipedes, tricycles; not the Sears
founded by Richard Sears

Selchow and Righter
New York, New York; Brooklyn, New York
1860s; toys, games; also jobbers

Shill, H. J.
Philadelphia, Pennsylvania
1870s; carriages

Shimer (William and Son) Company
Freemansburg, Pennsylvania
Mid-1870s; trains, toy banks, iron toys, etc.

Sigourney, J., and Company
Bristol, Connecticut
1850s; toy locomotives

Snow and Kingman
Boston, Massachusetts
1850s; hoops, wagons, wooden toys, etc.

South Bend Manufacturing Company
South Bend, Indiana
1874; croquet sets, etc.

Spaulding and Wilkens
Hastings, Michigan
1880s; croquet sets; one wonders if the
Spaulding Company, maker of athletic
equipment, sprung from this firm

Spelman and Payson
Albany, New York
1880s; blocks, puzzles

Springfield Manufacturing Company
Springfield, Vermont
1880s; toys

Standard Manufacturing Company
New Haven, Connecticut
1880s; mechanical toys

Steele, H. D.
Winchester, Connecticut
Mid-1850s; velocipedes, wagons, etc.

Stevens, J. and E.
Cromwell, Connecticut
1843 on; doll furniture, iron wheel toys,
penny toys, etc.; joined forces in the late
1860s with a George W. Brown to form
the American Toy Company

Stewart and Corbett
New York, New York
Late 1860s; rocking horses, sleds, carriages

Strobel and Wilkens
Cincinnati, Ohio
Late 1870s; toys; also jobbers

Tallman Toy Company
New York, New York
1890s; toys

Teel and Badet
South Bend, Indiana
Early 1880s; toys

Thomas Tin Company
New York, New York
1890s; toys

Thropp, C.
Plymouth, Connecticut
1880s; toys

Tiffany, Anson B.
Hartland, Connecticut
1860s; toys

Tower Toy Guild
South Hingham, Massachusetts
1830s; toy tools, doll furniture, wooden toys,
etc.; the Guild was a group of toy makers
who at one time or another participated
in its success and/or failure; most of the
toy makers in and around this town were
members at one time; later the Tower
Toy Company

Tower, William S.
South Hingham, Massachusetts
1830s; wooden toys, doll furniture

Toy Manufacturing Company
East Weare, New Hampshire
1870s; jumping jacks

Tricycle Manufacturing Company
Springfield, Ohio
1880s; tricycles, bicycles, wagons, etc.

Trenton Lock and Hardware Company
Trenton, New Jersey
Late 1870s; mechanical banks

Tuttle and Adams
Fitchburg, Massachusetts
Late 1870s; wooden toys, wheels

Union Carriage and Toy Company
Cleveland, Ohio
1890s; toys

Union Manufacturing Company
Clinton, Connecticut
1850s; toys

Union Manufacturing Company
Brooklyn, New York
1870s; steam engines, etc.

Union Toy Manufacturing Company
New York, New York
1890s; toys

Vanderbilt and McQueen
New York, New York
After Civil War; cradles, rocking horses,
other wood-turned pieces

Vanstone Manufacturing Company
Providence, Rhode Island
1890s; toys

Wakefield, Enoch H.
Boston, Massachusetts
Early 1850s; willow ware, wooden toys

Wallace, J.
North Weare, New Hampshire
1880s; toys

Warner Brothers
Bridgeport, Connecticut
Mid-1880s; baseballs

Watertown Carriage Company
Watertown, New York
Late 1880s; carriages; merged with Babcock
Motor Company, one of America's first
makers of electric cars; William J. Mills
was one of the pioneers in this field

Watkins and Roberts
New York, New York
1880s; toys

Watson and Rulafson
Bridgeport, Connecticut
1880s; iron toys

Weeden Company
New Bedford, Massachusetts
1880s; steam engines, toys

Weisman, W.
Cincinnati, Ohio
Early 1850s; toys

West and Lee Game Company
Worcester, Massachusetts
1870s; games etc.

Wheeler, A.
Brattleboro, Vermont
After Civil War; skates

Whigville Manufacturing Company
Burlington, Connecticut
Late 1840s; wooden toys

Wilder (Ezra and father)
South Hingham, Massachusetts
Father, 1860s; son, 1880s; wooden toys; both
were members of the Tower Toy Guild

Wilkens Toy Works
Keene, New Hampshire
Late 1880s; iron and steel toys; name
changed to Kingsbury Manufacturing
Company after 1894

Wilson Brothers Woodenware
and Toy Company
New York, New York
After Civil War to 1890s; games, carriages,
wooden toys, etc.

Winton Manufacturing Company
Binghamton, New York
Late 1880s; sleighs, carriages

Wood, J. C.
New York, New York
1880s; toys; also imported toys from Europe

Yaggy and Kinley
Chicago, Illinois
1880 to late 1880s; sleighs, bicycles, wagons,
etc.; Western Toy Company was another
name for this firm

Yearns and Smith
New York, New York
Late 1860s; kites

Note:
Obviously I have not listed all the manufacturers of toys, dolls, and those things that have to do with children. I hope I
have presented an overall selection of those fine people who made toys, either by hand or by machine, or who imported
such items from abroad. Perhaps I have erred in my research or omitted your favorite toy manufacturer. For this I am
sorry. My illustrious Grandfather was one of those who pioneered in the field of carriages and the horseless carriage.
God bless, Grand Papa!

TOY MUSEUMS IN THE UNITED STATES AND CANADA

Connecticut

Lyman Allyn Museum
100 Mohegan Avenue
New London

Toy Museum
Main Street
Oly Lyme

Isaac Stevens House
215 Main Street
Wethersfield

Florida

E. Martello Gallery/Museum
South Roosevelt Boulevard
Key West

Jacksonville Children's
Museum-at-the-fountain
Jacksonville

Museum of Yesterday's Toys
52 Saint George Street
Saint Augustine

The Museum of Old Dolls and Toys
Winter Haven

The Old Store Museum
Bravo Lane
Saint Augustine

The Lightner Museum
City Hall Bldg.
Saint Augustine

Illinois

Mercer County Museum
Southeast Second Avenue
Aledo

Historical Society of Quincy and
Adams County
425 South 12th Street
Quincy

Stephenson County Historical Society
1440 South Carroll Avenue
Freeport

Kankakee County Historical Society
Eighth Avenue at Water Street
Kankakee

Indiana

Tippecanoe County Historical Association
909 South Street
Lafayette

Kansas

Riley County Historical Society
Memorial Auditorium Building
Manhattan

Maryland

Allegany County Historical Society
218 Washington Street
Cumberland

Massachusetts

Society for the Preservation of
New England Antiquities
141 Cambridge Street
Boston

Children's Museum, Inc.
Russell's Mill Road
Dartmouth

The Nantucket Maria Mitchell Association
Vestal Street
Nantucket

Essex Institute
132 Essex Street
Salem

Michigan

Children's Museum
Detroit Public Schools
67 East Kirby Avenue
Detroit

Minnesota

Willard Bunnell House
Homer

Missouri

Powersite Museum
P.O. Box 77
Branson

New Hampshire

Old Store Museum
South Sutton

Museum of Old Dolls and Toys
Chesterfield Road
West Chesterfield

New Jersey

Boxwood Hall
1073 East Jersey Avenue
Elizabeth

Monmouth County Historical Association
70 Court Street
Freehold

Indian King Tavern
233 East King's Highway
Haddonfield

Morris Junior Museum
141 Madison Avenue
Morristown

Paramus Historical and Preservation Society
650 East Glen Avenue
Ridgewood

New York

Nassau County Historical Museum
Nassau County Park, Salisbury
East Meadow, Long Island

Prouty-Chew Museum
543 South Main Street
Geneva

Museum of the City of New York
1220 Fifth Avenue
New York

The New York Historical Society
170 Central Park West
New York

Seaman's Bank for Savings
The Maritime Collection
30 Wall Street
New York

Upper Susquehanna Historical
Society Museum
11 Ford Avenue
Oneonta

Southampton Historical Museum
Meeting House Lane
Southampton, Long Island

Southold Historical Society and Museum
Main Street
Southold, Long Island

Yorker Yankee Village
Irelandville Road
Watkins Glen

Ohio

Ross County Historical Society, Inc.
45 West Fifth Street
Chillicothe

Crestline Historical Society
211 North Thoman Street
Crestline

Emerine Collection
First National Bank
Fostoria

Ottawa County Historical Museum
Second and Adams Streets
Port Clinton

Pennsylvania

Perelman Antique Toy Museum
2nd and Spruce St.
Philadelphia

Karene Doll House
Knob Road and Lackawanna Trail
Mount Pocono

Rhode Island

Rhode Island Historical Society
52 Power Street
Providence

Texas

Crosby County Pioneer Memorial Museum
Pioneer Memorial Building
Crosbyton

Neill Museum
Fort Davis

Vermont

Walker Museum
Route 5
Fairlee

Sheldon Museum
1 Park Street
Middlebury

Shelburne Museum, Inc.
Shelburne Road
Shelburne

Wisconsin

Hoard Historical Museum
407 Merchants Avenue
Fort Atkinson

Douglas County Historical Museum
906 East Second Avenue
Superior

Canada

Bowmanville Museum
37 Silver Street
Bowmanville, Ontario

United Counties Museum
731 Second Street West
Cornwall, Ontario

Dundas Historical Society Museum
139 Park Street West
Dundas, Ontario

Victoria House Museum
512 Wellington Street
London, Ontario

Bytown Museum
Canal Locks, Rideau Canal
Ottawa, Ontario

Black Creek Pioneer Village
5 Jane Street
Toronto, Ontario

TOY PUBLICATIONS

Antique Toy World
3941 Belle Plaine
Chicago, Illinois 60618

Toy and Hobby World
735 Spring Street, N.W.
Atlanta, Georgia 30300

Toy Trader
157 Hagden Lane
Watford, Herts WDI 8LW, England

Toys
7c Carlton Drive
Putney, London SW 15, England

Toys
757 Third Avenue
New York, New York 10017

Toys and Playthings
146 Bates Road
Montreal, Quebec, Canada

Toys International
203-209 North Grower Street
London NW, England

PUBLICATIONS: ANTIQUES AND COLLECTIBLES

American Life Collector
Watkins Glen, New York 14891

Antique Monthly
Drawer 2
Tuscaloosa, Alabama 35401

Antiques
2 High Street
Wendover, Bucks, England

Antiques Magazine
551 Fifth Avenue
New York, New York 10017

Antiques Trader Weekly
Dubuque, Iowa 52001

Collectors News
Grundy Center, Iowa 50638

Antique Dealer
1115 Clifton Avenue
Clifton, New Jersey 07000

Hobbies Magazine
1006 South Michigan Avenue
Chicago, Illinois 60600

Maine Antique Dealer
Box 358
Waldoboro, Maine 04572

Antiques Journal
Dubuque, Iowa 52001

Hobbies to Enjoy
Box 2242
St. Louis, Missouri 63100

Southeast Trader
W. Columbia, South Carolina 29169

Spinning Wheel
Hanover, Pennsylvania 17331

Note: Obviously there are other publications and clubs about toys. If I have failed to list your publication or club, let me hear from you. I will include you in my next edition.

Subscription rates and publication quality vary, so write to them for a sample copy before you subscribe.